A TRIP TO
Leh Ladakh

I S Naveen

BLUEROSE PUBLISHERS
India | U.K.

Copyright © I S Naveen 2024

All rights reserved by author. No part of this publication may be reproduced, stored in a retrieval system or transmitted in any form or by any means, electronic, mechanical, photocopying, recording or otherwise, without the prior permission of the author. Although every precaution has been taken to verify the accuracy of the information contained herein, the publisher assumes no responsibility for any errors or omissions. No liability is assumed for damages that may result from the use of information contained within.

BlueRose Publishers takes no responsibility for any damages, losses, or liabilities that may arise from the use or misuse of the information, products, or services provided in this publication.

For permissions requests or inquiries regarding this publication, please contact:

BLUEROSE PUBLISHERS
www.BlueRoseONE.com
info@bluerosepublishers.com
+91 8882 898 898
+4407342408967

ISBN: 978-93-5989-978-7

Cover design: Rishav Rai
Typesetting: Rohit

First Edition: May 2024

Awesome trip to visit at least once in life

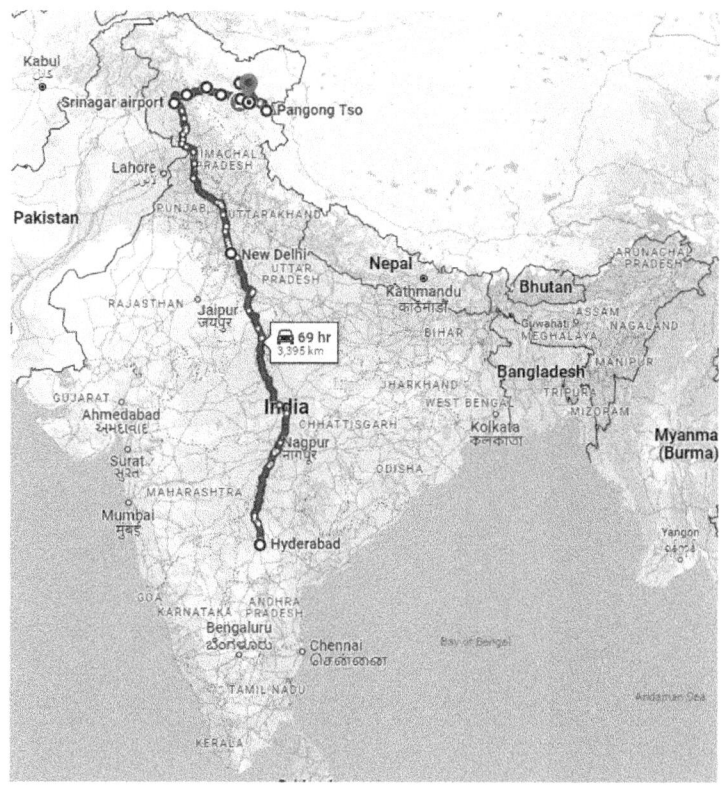

I extend my heartfelt gratitude to Gourav, Abhilash, Subhadeep, Pankaj, Dhanshree, Meenal and Shrutika for their invaluable contributions that have played a pivotal role in completing this book.

Contents

How Trip got planned 1
Hyderabad to SriNagar:first flight towards J&K 9
Kargil: long way to go 19
The Leh city: a dream of traveler 29
Ride towards Nubra Valley: culture exposure 45
Finally, The Pangong Lake: Multi-Weather ride 67
Adventurous ride to remember: Chang-LA Pass with
heavy snowfall 85
A view inside Leh city: Back to Hyderabad 101
Journeys Shared: Reflection of Fellow Travelers 121

How Trip got planned

दीर्घं स्वस्थं जीवनं यत्र सुखं भवति तत्र गच्छति

A long, healthy life goes where there is happiness

One day, I received a call from Abhilash who was in the midst of organizing a trip to Ladakh. He enthusiastically proposed, "Hey, how about embarking on a thrilling bike journey to Ladakh? We've already gathered a group of 5-6 people, and if you're up for it, we can chart out our own exciting itinerary."

The most recent adventure etched in my memory was our daring expedition to Patnitop, where we braved snow-filled valleys under the cloak of night. Another exhilarating journey that gets added to mind is my expedition to Leh-Ladakh. In an attempt to encapsulate the essence of this trip, I'll strive to articulate both the best and the most challenging moments of the experience.

Excitement and anticipation surged through me as my friend presented 2-3 meticulously crafted plans for our upcoming Leh visit. With a group of 6-7 eager individuals ready to embark on this adventure, my friend sought my confirmation, asking if I was prepared for the journey. Without hesitation, I replied, "Just book the ticket and keep me posted." At that moment, the desire to escape on this trip was overpowering. My mind was entangled in a web of issues, each one seemingly significant. I yearned for the serenity that a journey could provide, offering a temporary escape from the challenges that surrounded me. There are moments when circumstances are beyond our control, and in those times, I simply had to relinquish control and trust in destiny to guide this pivotal moment.

Alright, let's back to the Leh trip.

I was fully geared up and began preparations, gathering all the essentials for the trip, including cold weather gear and ensuring everything was set for the bike ride. A few days later, during a conference call to finalize the venue and route for our Leh expedition, one of my friends, subhadeep, expressed that he had encountered an issue and wouldn't be able to join us this time. Given his marital commitments, we empathized with his situation without a second thought. Our conversation shifted towards his life, delving into topics like marriage, travel, relationships, flat rentals, buying and selling, and more. Though I couldn't help but feel a tinge of disappointment after the call, I respected his decision—it was his call, and that was perfectly okay.

After a few more days, another friend, Pankaj, also had a change of heart, citing an issue that would prevent him from joining the trip. Abhilash also politely declined the invitation to join the trip, citing another pressing commitment. At this point, you might be wondering, "What now?" It was getting increasingly challenging to sustain the momentum of our trip plans. I finally conceded, saying, "Okay, let's plan for next year."

As fate would have it, our smartphones, diligently tracking every aspect of our lives through our conversations, started inundating me with links related to the Leh trip. Intrigued, I delved into the trip details and routes. The notion of embarking on a solo trip to Leh-Ladakh took center stage in my thoughts, becoming my primary search.

One day, a message popped up on WhatsApp, asking, "You registered for the Leh trip through our link. Are you still interested?" Curious, I inquired about the feasibility and safety of solo biking to Leh. To my delight, the agent responded with a resounding affirmation, assuring me that it was not only possible but also safe.

Me: "Could you inform me of the available travel dates? I'm interested in the first week of June."

Agent: "Certainly, we have two available dates: June 2nd and June 8th."

Me: "Which of these dates has a higher number of travelers already registered?"

Agent: "For June 2nd, we already have a team of around 9-10 people traveling together. We are looking for two more to finalize the group for this trip. On June 8th, there are only two travelers at the moment."

Me: "In the event that more travelers do not signup for the June 8th date, would the trip be cancelled?"

Agent: "No, rest assured, the trip will proceed as scheduled even if it's just one person."

His response certainly took me by surprise. After conducting some research, I discovered that while they may assure us the trip will proceed regardless of the number of participants, there is a possibility of cancellation if the turnout is too low on a given date. I've also been dealing with trip cancellation issues previously, so I wanted to minimize any risk of this happening again. With that in mind, I decided to choose the June 2nd date, as the likelihood of cancellation seemed significantly lower.

Me: "I'd like to book for June 2nd. Could you inform me about the payment details?"

Agent: "You can secure your booking by paying 50 percent of the total cost."

The following day, I proceeded with the booking despite harboring some reservations about potentially falling victim to a scam. However, I found some solace in the fact that I had already secured my flight ticket from Hyderabad to

Delhi. With this in mind, I considered a backup plan of visiting Rishikesh in case the trip turned out to be fraudulent and I ended up losing my money.

In the following days, my friend, Ankit Tyagi, inquired about the status of my Leh trip and whether it had been canceled. I informed him, "I've already made the booking and paid as well." His surprise was palpable and he began contemplating joining me. Like me, he was wary of potential fraud, so he decided to do some online research about the trip advisor. After considering all factors, he finally agreed to accompany me on the trip.

Now, both Ankit and I were booked for the journey, and cancellation was no longer an option. We were committed to this adventure.

We meticulously compiled our list of essentials and commenced the process of gathering everything we needed. The much-anticipated 1st of June finally arrived after what seemed like an eternity.

Ankit chimed in, "Hey, buddy, I've double-checked the list, and everything's packed in the bag. Jackets, 5-6 pairs of socks, gloves, goggles, but how many pants, shirts, innerwear, cold caps, biking necessities..."

I couldn't shake the feeling that our checklist wasn't quite comprehensive, and it dawned on me that we might overlook something crucial. Nevertheless, I embraced the adventure with a sense of readiness, acknowledging that, "We'll deal with whatever comes our way on this trip."

After a day at the office, I decided to unwind by sharing a beer with my friends in the comfort of my room. As the evening progressed, I meticulously gathered all the items listed for our upcoming trip and stowed them away in my bag. Confident in my organizational skills, I believed that I had successfully accounted for every essential on the list.

Meanwhile, Ankit took charge of booking a cab for our journey and conscientiously weighed his luggage to ensure

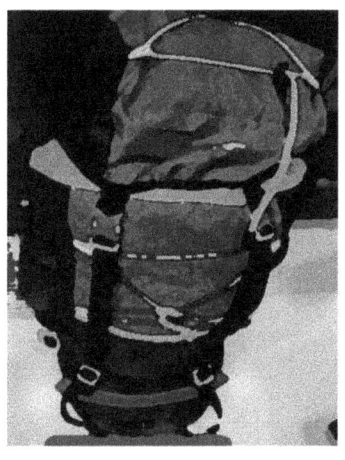

it met the airline's check-in regulations. The scale indicated a weight just shy of the maximum limit, instilling in me a newfound confidence that he, too, had diligently packed the majority of the required items. The thought echoed in my mind, "It means he must have covered most bases, even if I happened to overlook something."

With the cab at our doorstep, we embarked on our journey from our flat to the airport. Upon arrival, the late-night ambiance of the airport was surprisingly serene, with fewer crowds milling about. Swiftly navigating through security checks and the check-in process, we found ourselves with a generous amount of spare time before our scheduled flight to Delhi.

Not ones to let the opportunity pass, we decided to explore a newly opened restaurant at the Hyderabad airport. There, we ordered a round of beers and indulged in a leisurely dinner. The effects of that beer left me feeling not only refreshed but also entirely prepared and in high spirits for the adventures that awaited us on our impending trip.

Hyderabad to SriNagar: first flight towards J&K

सर्वं अनुभवः, सर्वं यात्रा, जीवनं एकं अनन्तं सौन्दर्यम्

Everything is an experience, everything is a journey, life is one endless beauty.

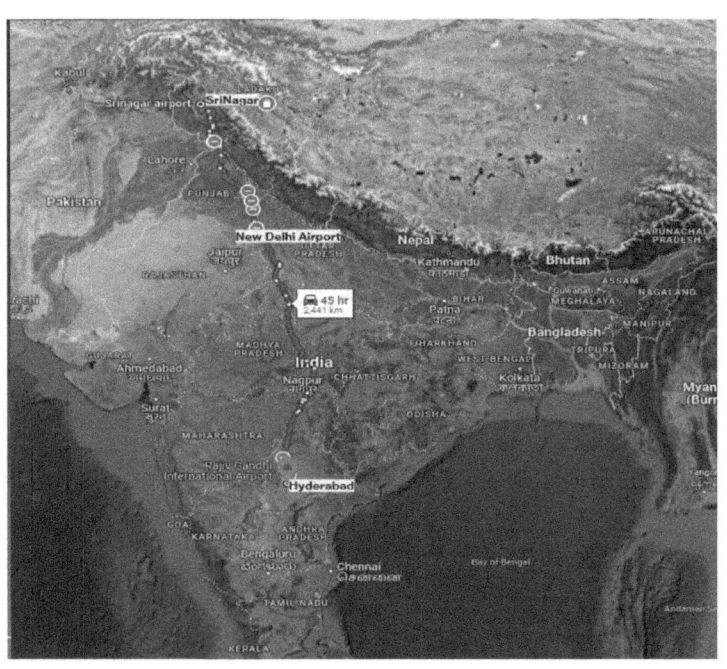

In adherence to my customary travel routine, I smoothly navigated the boarding process, finding solace in the familiar embrace of my designated seat. For this particular journey, I had taken proactive measures by downloading a curated selection of movies, ensuring a source of entertainment throughout the flight. Making efficient use of my time, I indulged in one of these films, allowing the hours to pass seamlessly as we journeyed towards Delhi. As anticipated, our arrival in Delhi was punctual, marking the transition to the next phase of our travel—a flight to Srinagar, scheduled for the early morning hours at 5:45 am. With a substantial 4-5 hours to spare, we found ourselves with an opportunity to explore the interim surroundings.

Fueled by a sense of curiosity, I opted to venture into the Delhi lounge, a first-time experience for me. Regrettably, my initial enthusiasm was tempered by the sight of a considerable queue, underscoring the challenges faced by this lounge in one of India's busiest airports. Notably, Delhi Airport, renowned for its bustling activity, offered only this lounge option for general passengers equipped with a valid credit card. Despite the extended wait of 30-45 minutes, we eventually secured two coveted spots within the lounge, utilizing the time to unwind and relish a delicious snack with coffee.

Yoga pose, Delhi Airport

Departing the lounge with a comfortable buffer before our boarding time, we embarked on a leisurely stroll toward Gate 44A. Along the way, we seized the opportunity to capture the vibrant allure of the airport's floral arrangements in a series of photographs. The statues depicting yoga poses immediately caught my eye. I used to practice a form of yoga called 'Surya Namaskar,' which made these statues particularly intriguing to me.

Noting that Gates 42 to 46 were situated downstairs, we descended a level, eventually rediscovering Gate 44 in the same downward direction. Despite the slight detour, the additional minutes afforded us a chance to appreciate the airport's architectural nuances before reaching the gate, ensuring we were present for the boarding process with ample time to spare.

As per the information from our travel advisor, we were scheduled to share the flight with a group of nine other travelers. As Ankit and I boarded the plane and settled into our assigned seats, we noticed an empty window seat. This seat, according to the flight manifest, was reserved for a person from the other group who had yet to arrive.

As the scheduled departure time had already passed, the situation began to grow tense. A part of me started to worry that they might miss the flight due to their tardiness. The air was filled with anticipation, and the suspense was almost palpable.

Suddenly, the tranquility of the cabin was broken by the hurried entrance of eight individuals, presumably the other part of our group. They were in a state of disarray, engaging in a fervent discussion about their missing ninth member, Meenal, over the phone. It became clear that the individual who was supposed to be seated next to the window was unfortunately not able to make the flight. This unexpected turn of events added a layer of complexity to the beginning of our journey. They settled comfortably into their seats, engrossed in a discussion about their missing companion. Unaware that we were traveling together, I observed their conversation. While I was pleased to have secured the window seat, I couldn't help but feel a pang of sympathy for the absent individual. Having experienced similar situations before, I understood the frustration and inconvenience it could cause.

As the flight took off, I delved into another movie, gradually succumbing to the allure of sleep within the next few minutes. Abruptly, a voice interrupted my peaceful slumber, urging, "See the scenes outside." Startled awake, I gazed out of the window to behold an awe-inspiring panorama. The sight was nothing short of breathtaking—a tranquil expanse of mountains encircling a river, pristine peaks adorned with snow , all seamlessly interconnected. It was

SriNagar mountains – flight view

as if the mountains themselves were conveying a profound message: "Be united and extraordinary; nurture the essence of nature within you."

The scene unfolding before me defied description. It resembled a living tableau akin to the images I had explored on Google Maps before embarking on this journey. Scattered clouds and the gentle embrace of the sun added an extra layer of serenity, all encapsulated within a single frame. The sheer beauty and harmony of nature were indescribable, resonating with a message of unity and appreciation.

Our descent into Srinagar marked the culmination of this mesmerizing aerial journey. The Srinagar airport itself, ensconced amidst valleys, hills, and snow-capped mountains, continued the theme of natural grandeur, serving as a fitting introduction to the enchanting landscapes that awaited us in this pleasing destination.

Stepping off the plane, the murmurs of our fellow travelers discussing the missing person greeted my ears. They were also speculating about us, as we hadn't yet met. Ankit and I made our way to the baggage claim area, where we introduced ourselves and engaged in conversation about our journey from Delhi to Srinagar. They recounted how their friend had narrowly missed the flight, arriving at the boarding gate just two minutes too late as the door was closing. Since it was the first flight of the morning, the flight operated on a strict schedule, with boarding doors closing 25 minutes prior to departure. Despite this hiccup, we were all eager and excited about our upcoming adventures exploring the streets of Srinagar, starting from Dal Lake and heading towards Kargil.

Stepping out of the airport, our anticipation was met with the sight of our traveler van patiently waiting just beyond the terminal's confines. Gathering our belongings, we efficiently secured our luggage atop the van before settling into our seats. Choosing a window seat, I sought to absorb the palpable essence of Kashmir's natural beauty. This marked my second sojourn to the region, a return after a hiatus spanning almost 18-19 years. The last time I visited this place was around 2005, and memories of that trip flooded back as I stepped into familiar surroundings. The sights and sounds seemed both new and familiar, triggering a sense of nostalgia. As I walked around, I noticed how much had changed since my last visit—the buildings seemed different, the streets busier, yet the essence of the place remained unchanged. My mind wandered back to those earlier days, recalling the adventures and experiences I had during that time. The familiarity of Kashmir's nature enveloped me, from the distinctive wooden homes to the triangular-shaped rooftops that dotted the landscape. Each street offered a unique view of the surrounding mountains, while Indian flags fluttered proudly, seamlessly weaving into the fabric of the captivating scenery.

Dal Lake, Kashmir

As life unfolded around us, the streets came alive with scenes of schoolchildren marching proudly, their hands adorned with Indian flags. Locals traversed the roads with contagious smiles, embodying the warmth and camaraderie of the community. Yet, amid the seemingly idyllic setting, the presence of security forces served as a reminder of the complex dynamics that shape the city's narrative.

Our journey eventually led us to the heart of Kashmir—the iconic Dal Lake. A visual masterpiece, the lake reflected the sky with remarkable clarity, mirroring the majestic mountains that surrounded it. As our van leisurely traversed the periphery of Dal Lake for the next half-hour, I found myself captivated by the serene grandeur unfolding before my eyes.

The culmination of this lovely journey brought us to a brief stop at a Dhaba for breakfast, providing a welcome opportunity to disembark and immerse ourselves in the tranquility of The Dal Lake of Kashmir. Against this backdrop, we seized the moment to capture memories, pausing to take numerous photographs that encapsulated the essence of our arrival in this captivating destination.

In a serendipitous encounter, Ankit and I found ourselves in the company of eight fellow travelers who would become our companions for the remainder of our expedition through the enchanting landscapes of Leh. During our initial rendezvous, conversations naturally gravitated towards the individual who had missed the flight and the planning of our upcoming journey. Seeking sustenance at a local Dhaba, I opted for a serving of aloo paratha accompanied by a steaming cup of coffee—a modest repast that served as a necessary source of energy for the impending journey through the undulating hills.

An hour later, our traveler rumbled to life, setting forth on the winding roads to our next destination. Accompanying our driver was his brother, who, much to our delight, decided to infuse the journey with the soulful melodies of old Bollywood tunes from the 90s. Having traversed through the night, a collective wave of weariness swept through the group, and one by one, my fellow travelers succumbed to the rhythmic lullaby of the music, drifting into a restful sleep.

Yet, amid the lull of slumber, wakefulness lingered within me, prompting a conversation with the driver's brother. A soul close in age, he had recently completed his graduation and harbored a profound curiosity about life's possibilities beyond the borders of Kashmir. Our discourse delved into his aspirations for further studies and the exploration of opportunities that lay beyond familiar horizons. The unfolding narrative led to discussions about the prevailing conditions in Kashmir. His account painted a picture of positive transformation, with an increasing sense of acceptance in Unity of the Nation, fostering feelings of safety and independence in pursuing diverse careers.

As the van traversed the diverse landscape, he eloquently unfolded the tapestry of cultural distinctions between Kashmir and Jammu—the nuances in language, culinary preferences, traditional attire, and the variations in weather that define each region. This journey to Leh marked his inaugural exploration of the famed destination, aligning with our own, and he generously shared insights into the evolving dynamics of the region. Eventually, the rhythmic hum of the van and the soothing exchange of stories lulled me into a contemplative slumber, the landscape unfolding amidst tales of cultural diversity and shared dreams.

Kargil: long way to go

जीवनस्य यात्रा विविधा अस्ति, प्रत्येकं अनुभवः अद्वितीयः अस्ति
Life's journey is diverse, each experience unique.

Our journey continued towards the next district, Kangan, along the scenic route. Around noon, we made a pit stop for tea and snacks. The landscape unfolded before us, offering a crystal-clear view of the majestic mountains, with our van seemingly in pursuit of their grandeur. Nestled in this beautiful setting was a local shop boasting an array of jackets, shawls, and other indigenous items. Intrigued, I tried on a few jackets, though they were slightly oversized, prompting me to forego a purchase. The spot presented an opportunity to linger a while, relishing the chance to partake in local shopping and savoring some delectable snacks. After indulging in shopping and enjoying some snacks for about half an hour, we were rejuvenated and ready to continue our journey. The brief break had lifted our spirits, and we were eager to explore more. As we set off again, the anticipation of what lay ahead filled us with excitement.

Our eagerly awaited destination, Sonmarg, beckoned on the horizon, and the journey unfolding towards it had its own mesmerizing charm. Along the route, a river accompanied us, its harmonious flow providing a soothing undertone to the music playing in the background. The collective mood on our journey shifted, and a newfound joy permeated the van as everyone began to immerse themselves in the melodies and the stunning vistas outside. Each member of our group had embarked on this venture to escape the bustling cacophony of city life, seeking solace and rejuvenation in the lap of nature.

Sonmarg

As we traversed through the enchanting landscapes of Sonmarg, our excitement soared to unparalleled heights. Majestic mountains, adorned with pristine blankets of snow, stood as sentinels, while a meandering river flowed gracefully in the valley below. Towering trees added to the scenic beauty, creating a landscape that was nothing short of a visual feast. A stop at a quaint tea shop became a delightful interlude, where we indulged in the warmth of steaming Maggi and seized the opportunity to capture the beauty around us in photographs, etching these moments into our memories.

My anticipation for the upcoming motorcycle rides intensified, especially as the first droplets of rain started to fall, accompanied by a gentle touch of snowfall—a rare and exhilarating occurrence, especially for those accustomed to the routine of bustling cities like Pune or Hyderabad.

Our astute driver, sensing the group's eagerness, advised against lingering too long, emphasizing that the subsequent leg of our journey promised even more captivating sights—mountains blanketed in pristine snow and a perceptible

drop in temperature. Eager to embrace the anticipated adventure, we all adorned ourselves with jackets, preparing for the crisp chill that awaited, and eagerly boarded the van, poised for the next chapter in our extraordinary expedition through the picturesque landscapes of Sonmarg.

We found ourselves traversing the shadowy expanse of the Ladakh road, weaving through a forested region. The surroundings exuded a serene calmness, with sparse human presence in the valleys. The only concern, however, lay in the winding roads that snaked through the valleys, causing a few to experience a sense of dizziness. The discomfort dissipated as we reached our next stop, a place that would render the entire group breathless – the Zojila Pass. This was the juncture where we anticipated encountering an awe-inspiring 15-20 feet of ice on the road. Arriving in the next half-hour, we disembarked and marveled at the breathtaking landscape that unfolded before us.

A biting cold wind swept through the air, penetrating our beings, prompting us to tightly cover our ears to shield ourselves from the chilling gusts. Amidst this chilly ambiance, the Zojila Pass showcased an enthralling display of ice-related activities on the snowy mountains. The sight of ice-mobiles navigating the frozen terrain sparked a sense of adventure within Ankit and me. Undeterred by the prospect of going solo, we approached one of the guides to inquire about the cost of riding the ice-mobile. Negotiations ensued, resulting in a subsidized rate that enticed four other individuals to join our daring escapade.

Seated atop a gleaming ice-mobile, with a motor guide occupying the back seat, we embarked on a thrilling ride. As the motor gained momentum, the cold wind whistled past, and the sensation of the mountain's icy peak enveloped us. Accelerating to the middle of the mountain, the motor came to a halt, signaling our designated resting spot. Disembarking, we found ourselves surrounded by a pristine blanket of snow, stretching from top to bottom, left to right, with nothing but the chill wind as our companion. Amidst laughter and shared moments captured in photographs, I relished the frigid air—a stark contrast to the warmth of the city that I had grown accustomed to.

Venturing to a quiet corner, I settled down on the snow, contemplating life, work, and the world around me. In the sudden stillness, my thoughts ceased, and I surrendered to the tranquility of nature. The crisp cold air invigorated my senses, prompting me to linger a while longer until the others completed their photo sessions.

Returning from the snow-covered escapade, the thrill of the ice-mobile ride still tingling in our veins, we settled back into our van's comfortable seats. The warmth enveloping us contrasted beautifully with the chilly adventure we had just experienced. As the rhythmic hum of our traveler resumed, so did the lively exchange of stories and laughter among us. The melodies of our chosen music filled the van, creating a lively atmosphere that complemented the camaraderie forged during our icy escapade.

Our next destination, Dras, awaited us, promising new vistas and experiences. As we embraced the cozy ambiance within the van, the sense of anticipation for the wonders that lay ahead infused the air. The van meandered through the enchanting landscapes, carrying us toward the next chapter of our Leh Ladakh odyssey, leaving behind the frosty memories of Zojila Pass as a testament to the exhilarating journey that lay ahead.

En route to Dras, the landscape unfolded in a mesmerizing display of diverse mountain formations—some cloaked in pristine snow, others adorned with long trees, leafless branches, and rugged rocks, both black and red. The scenic panorama captivated our senses, offering a visual symphony of nature's artistry. By around 5 pm, our van came to a halt at the Kargil War Memorial, its name resonating with the historical echoes of conflict in Kargil. Luckily, we arrived just in time before the gates closed for the day.

The memorial stood as a solemn tribute, guarded by uniformed figures at every turn. Our entry required a brief verification of Aadhar card IDs, and upon entering, the fluttering Indian flag against the backdrop of mountains invoked a sense of pride. Standing before the memorial, an army captain gathered the tourists, recounting the events of the Kargil War. His narrative unfolded the tale of Pakistan's intrusion into Indian territory, the capture of strategic hilltops like Tiger Hills, and the subsequent heroic efforts of the Indian army to reclaim these positions. The sacrifices of great personalities like Major Vikram Batra and Manoj, among others, stirred a profound sense of guilt for not knowing more about these valiant souls.

Entering the memorial hall, we encountered a repository of captured weapons, war memorabilia, and stories of bravery by our Majors and Captains. A surge of pride and patriotism engulfed me as I reflected on the sacrifices made by these soldiers. A poignant quotation etched in the hall resonated deeply: "When you go home, tell them of us and say 'for your tomorrow, we gave our today'." This sentiment left an ineradicable mark on my heart.

A documentary showcased the valiant tales of our armed forces, an experience I deemed essential for every Indian. With a heavy yet grateful heart, we exited the memorial. A local shop beckoned, offering the famed "*pahado wali maggi*" that proved to be a delectable treat amidst the chilly winds. The frigid air swiftly cooled the piping hot maggi, a testament to kargil's unique weather.

As our van embarked on the journey to Kargil city, I found solace in sleep, contemplating the war memorial and the remarkable personalities it commemorated. By 8:30 pm,

Kargil's distinctive cityscape came into view—a world nestled among historical valleys. Despite the late hour, the sun's lingering glow cast an early evening aura over Kargil, creating a surreal ambiance.

Our night's stay at the Hill Town hotel was a serene experience, complete with the comfort of hot water. After freshening up, we gathered for a delightful dinner that surpassed expectations. I indulged in a feast, combining lunch, snacks, and dinner. Post-meal, Ankit and I ventured out to explore Kargil, but the city had already embraced tranquility by 9-9:30 pm. Returning to our room, we succumbed to sleep, drifting into dreams against the backdrop of Kargil's unique charm.

Kargil City

The Leh city: a dream of traveler

शान्तिं आलिंगयन्तु, अनन्तं अन्वेषणं कुर्वन्तु, आनन्दस्य आविष्कारं कुर्वन्तु
Embrace serenity, explore endlessly, discover joy

I roused from my slumber early the next morning, greeted by the sight of the sun ascending just beyond the mountains. The room, equipped with a window that opened to the mountainous expanse, ushered in the tranquility of a peaceful morning. Golden rays of sunlight traversed the mountains, casting a warm glow that bathed the entire city in a rosy hue. Entranced by this breathtaking spectacle, I spent some quiet moments basking in the beauty of the sunrise and the majestic mountains.

Eventually, I descended the stairs and sought a cup of tea to accompany the burgeoning day. Sipping on the warm elixir, I returned to my room, relishing the soothing effects of hot water. With plans to be prepared by 9, I commenced my morning routine, packing my bags and organizing my belongings. By 8:30, we had all vacated our rooms, congregating at the breakfast table to commence our day. The breakfast spread was nothing short of amazing, and I found myself indulging in a hearty meal, including milk, eggs, and parathas, setting the tone for a day filled with adventure.

Embarking on our journey from Kargil, we set out a tad behind schedule, our next destination being the Mulbekh Monastery, approximately 36 kilometers away. The route unfolded with a panormic conversation between mountains, each peak and valley telling its own unique story. The roads, remarkably clean, accommodated fellow travelers sharing the scenic drive. Our driver and his brother curated a nostalgic ambiance, a playlist of '90s songs accompanying us on this mountainous expedition.

Arriving at Mulbekh, the landscape seemed to cradle an ancient village nestled in the hills. The sparse population added to the quaint charm, with a few shops catering to the passing tourists. My immediate focus was on the monastery, an emblem of Tibetan artistry, surrounded by devout Buddhists engaged in prayer. A nominal entry fee of 30 rupees granted me access, and as I stepped inside, I was met with a captivating sight—a 30-feet tall statue of Lord Buddha intricately carved into the rock. Dating back to 100-200 BC, the statue demanded a reverent upward gaze to fully appreciate its grandeur. The serene ambiance within, punctuated by the rhythmic routines of the attending priests, prompted me to pause, offering prayers for global peace.

Surrounded by mountains, one couldn't help but marvel at the monumental effort exerted by ancient craftsmen in creating this timeless statue. The setting added a unique layer of beauty to the already stunning mountainous landscape. The cultural phenomenon of offering prayers was a sight to behold. As I observed, everyone around me was engaged in silent prayer, their faces serene and peaceful, illuminated by gentle smiles. It was a moment of tranquility amidst the bustling surroundings. Inspired by the atmosphere, I too offered my prayers, joining in with a sense of reverence and calm. As I stepped out, I carried with me the peaceful energy of that moment, feeling grateful for the experience.

Exiting the monastery, we captured multiple scenic memories, reboarded our van, and eagerly set forth toward our next destination, leaving behind the echoes of ancient craftsmanship etched into the hills.

As we journeyed forward, the wind began to pick up, carrying with it a chill that seemed to seep into our bones. It whipped through the air with increased speed, causing a noticeable drop in temperature. Despite the cold, there was a certain exhilaration in feeling the brisk wind against our skin, a reminder of the raw power of nature. We adjusted our clothing, pulling our jackets tighter around us, and continued on, braving the elements as we pressed on with our journey. Our expedition led us to our first high-altitude destination on the journey—Namikala. The landscape unfolded, revealing a breathtaking series of mountains, each unique in its formation yet seamlessly connected. The well-maintained roads paved the way for a smooth and enjoyable journey, with our destination on the horizon. By 11 am, we arrived at Namikala, situated at an impressive 12,198 feet. A popular stopover for travelers, it welcomed us with a map showcasing the intricate network of roads leading to Leh and the surrounding villages, along with the key attractions for tourists.

A mountainous panorama stretched before us, and I couldn't resist the urge to ascend to the half-summit of one towering peak. Scaling the heights, I embraced the invigorating mountain air, surrounded by the wonders of nature and a series of majestic peaks. A profound sense of joy welled up within me. As I reached a spot with a clear signal, I seized the opportunity to call a few friends, sharing the mesmerizing scenery and planning future trips together. Sitting there, I soaked in the serene atmosphere until my fellow travelers signaled that it was time to move on.

With more destinations to explore and places to cover on our journey to Leh, we resumed our adventure, fueled by the memories of Namikala's lofty beauty and the anticipation of what lay ahead. Next stop at Fotu La heights during our journey to Lamayuru was a captivating interlude amid the grandeur of the mountains. The cold wind, though piercing, couldn't diminish the allure of the breathtaking landscape that unfolded before us. With a sense of exhilaration, we braved the elements long enough to capture a series of photographs, each frame freezing a moment in the chilly embrace of Fotu La. As we retreated into the shelter of our van, the memory of this brief encounter lingered, adding to the tapestry of our adventurous expedition through the high-altitude wonders of the region.

As we immersed ourselves in the captivating aura of Lumayuru Monastery, the intricate details within its sacred walls painted a tapestry of cultural richness. The chilly breeze whispered ancient tales as we strolled through, admiring the distinct pillars, the vibrant wall paintings that seemed to echo with history, and the serenity emanating from the Buddha sculptures.

Ascending a staircase toward the monastery's roof, we were greeted by a panoramic view that transcended the ordinary. The Lumayuru village sprawled below, a harmonious blend of terracotta structures against the backdrop of majestic mountains. Capturing the essence of this stunning scene, we clicked photographs, each frame encapsulating the timeless beauty of Ladakh.

Lumayuru

Inside, a small temple nestled within the valley offered a moment of spiritual serenity amidst the natural grandeur. As we explored further, the monastery's unique charm unfolded, revealing not just a place of worship but a living testament to the enduring legacy of Ladakh's cultural heritage.

The generous hospitality extended within the monastery included complimentary local tea, a gesture that underscored the warmth of this sacred space. Though the taste might have been unfamiliar, the experience of sipping tea within the walls of Lumayuru Monastery was a memorable aspect of our visit.

After bidding adieu to the spiritual sanctuary, we returned to our van, savoring snacks from Hyderabad that added a touch of familiarity to this faraway adventure. Lingering for a while, we absorbed the tranquility of Lumayuru's surroundings, imprinting the moment in our memories before embarking on the journey to our next destination.

Embarking on our next leg of the journey with empty stomachs, we set our sights on Nurla and the promise of a satisfying meal at a local dhaba or hotel. The anticipation for culinary delights fueled our conversation, still steeped in the awe-inspiring views and architectural wonders of Lumayuru.

Upon reaching Nurla, our driver expertly pulled over near a Punjabi hotel, where the aroma of delectable dishes beckoned us inside. We eagerly placed orders for parathas, rice with dal, and some flavorful fried rice. Ankit, a devoted black coffee enthusiast, found his elixir on the menu and promptly requested a cup. The brewing process, though seemingly eternal, concluded with Ankit savoring every sip of his coffee, a surge of newfound energy coursing through him. His enthusiasm reached a point where he proclaimed his readiness to take the wheel for the remaining journey of the day.

To channel Ankit's energized spirit away from driving in the valley, we collectively relegated him to the back seat. Little did we know that the following day would mark the commencement of our solo bike ride, a prospect that had been playing out vividly in my mind, simultaneously thrilling and exhilarating me throughout the journey thus far. The excitement of the impending bike ride lingered in my thoughts, promising an adventure that would weave its own tales through the winding roads of Ladakh.

Following our delightful meal at Nurla, we set off towards the Sangam River. This location is of significant importance as it is the confluence of two major rivers, the Indus and the Zolanski. The journey offered us a spectacular view of the

Sangam valleys, a sight that was nothing short of breathtaking.

Amidst this, one of our group members received a call from Meenal, the girl who had missed her flight to Srinagar. She had managed to take a direct flight to Leh and was planning to rendezvous with us at the Sangam River, joining us for the remainder of the trip. Her imminent arrival sparked a flurry of conversation within the group, with everyone speculating about her feelings and experiences.

Along the banks of the Indus River, we were treated to a breathtaking display of nature's artistry as the river flowed gracefully, adorned in hues of lush green. The transparency of the water was such that we could peer into its depths, revealing a world teeming with aquatic life. Our leisurely stroll, coupled with animated conversation, allowed us to soak in the beauty of the Sangam Valleys until our path led us to the confluence point of the Sangam River.

At this juncture, Meenal, eagerly awaiting the arrival of her group, greeted them with a beaming smile that spoke of relief and contentment. The serene ambiance surrounding us bore witness to not only the natural wonders but also to the hushed murmurs of discussions. Conversations echoed about the intricacies of Meenal's missed flight, creating an air of curiosity that added an unexpected layer to our exploration of this tranquil haven.

From the elevated vantage point of the road, a captivating panorama unfolded before me—two majestic rivers, the Indus and Zanskar, gracefully converging at Sangam. The distinct colors of each river, one a vibrant green and the other a serene bluish hue, melded seamlessly at this confluence. These rivers, having traversed vast distances from lofty mountains and through attractive valleys, appeared to carry the essence of multiple landscapes into the embrace of Sangam.

Sangam of Indus and Zanskar river

The spectacle of this natural union, where mountains and rivers coexisted harmoniously, left an indelible impression. The merging of valleys and rivers at Sangam was a testament to the awe-inspiring beauty crafted by nature. In the midst of this breathtaking scenery, our cameras were put to good use, capturing the essence of Sangam and the surrounding mountains.

With Meenal's arrival, our group was now complete. Gathering into the same van, we embarked on the next leg of our journey, headed towards the intriguing Magnetic Hill, eager to unravel more wonders that the region had to offer. The journey from Sangam to the Magnetic Hill, though relatively short at just half an hour, was filled with anticipation and curiosity. As we drove, I delved into the details of the magnetic impact of the hills, immersing myself in the fascinating descriptions I had read online. Despite the vivid explanations, I couldn't shake a hint of skepticism until we arrived and experienced it firsthand. Discussing the natural phenomenon along the way only heightened our excitement. Upon reaching the Magnetic Hill, we were greeted by a surreal landscape. Large, natural magnets exerted their force, creating a palpable effect. The road was marked with a clearly defined zone where the magnetic impact was most intense. Standing within this zone, it felt as though gravity itself was being defied, a sensation that had to be experienced to be truly understood. As I stood within the demarcated zone, the peculiar force pulling objects backward seemed to defy the laws of physics, creating a surreal atmosphere between the two imposing mountains. The lack of any discernible incline on the straight road only heightened the mystery, leaving me in awe of the magnetic anomalies at play. Every vehicle that comes to a stop in the designated area experiences a remarkable phenomenon: it begins to move uphill, apparently pulled by an unseen force. This unusual effect, often attributed to gravity, propels the vehicles in the opposite direction at a steady pace of around 20 km/h. It's a surreal experience that defies conventional explanation, leaving visitors in awe of the mysteries of nature.

The landscape, bathed in the soft glow of twilight, accentuated the contrast between the shadowy, light-absorbing mountain and the rugged expanse of the desert-like terrain. It was as though nature itself was orchestrating a cosmic dance, with the Magnetic Hill as the stage.

Amidst the gravitational mysteries, the distant hum of ATV engines drew my attention. Intrigued by the prospect of exploring the surroundings in a different way, I joined Ankit in securing an ATV for ourselves. The vibrations beneath me as I navigated the rocky terrain, coupled with the swirling dust in the mountain air, added a tactile and immersive dimension to the already exhilarating adventure.

Magnetic Hills

The interplay of light and shadows, the distant murmur of the rivers, and the magnetic pull that seemed to linger in the air created an otherworldly ambiance. Riding the ATV through this captivating landscape felt like a journey through a dreamscape, where reality and illusion coexisted in perfect harmony.

As the stars began to dot the night sky, casting a celestial glow over the mountains, I couldn't help but marvel at the serendipity of discovering the Magnetic Hill—a place where the ordinary rules of nature seemed to take a captivating detour.

As fatigue settled in, prompting our collective decision to head back to Leh, a serendipitous opportunity presented itself on the way—the revered Gurudwara Pathar Sahib. Eager to take advantage of this spiritual pause, we made a pit stop, refreshing ourselves by washing our tired legs before stepping into the sanctified premises of the Gurudwara Pathar sahib.

This sacred site held the historical resonance of a Guru Sahib engaged in meditation, an event where a colossal demon hurled a massive stone at the revered figure. Astonishingly, upon impact, the stone transformed into wax, assuming the very shape of the Guru Sahib's back. Witnessing this miraculous occurrence, the malevolent force underwent a profound change, embracing devotion to the Guru.

The air was filled with the joyful noise of children playing around. Someone gently reminded them to quiet down. Pratiek stepped up, taking charge, and calmly settled them, granting us a moment of silence. We sat together, enjoying the tranquility of our surroundings, before finally venturing out of the peaceful premises. The aura of positivity and spiritual energy enveloped us as we spent a contemplative half-hour in this hallowed space. Partaking in the communal feast of kheer offered as langar heightened the sense of communal connection. Emerging from the Gurudwara, we were treated to the most delectable tea of the entire journey, a delightful surprise that lingered on our taste buds.

Gurudwara Pathar Sahib

Savoring the warmth of the tea, we indulged in capturing the essence of the surroundings through numerous photographs before returning to our van. As dusk settled, we made our way to Leh, our destination for the night. As evening approached in the metro city, the sun was expected to set, casting a warm glow over the bustling streets. However, in Leh City, the sun remained high in the sky, its rays still strong and radiant. The discrepancy in the timing of sunset between the two locations was striking, highlighting the unique geographical and climatic features of Leh. The sun's lingering presence painted the city in a golden light, creating a surreal and captivating scene that contrasted with the approaching dusk in the metro city. Arriving at our hotel around 8 PM, we checked into our rooms. Meenal, bubbling with excitement about exploring the Leh market, set out for an evening adventure, while Ankit and I chose to revel in the serenity of our room.

The following day held the promise of solo bike riding adventures around Leh and Ladakh, adding an anticipatory thrill to the calm of the present moment. As the night deepened, we found ourselves immersed in reflections of the day's encounters, the spiritual energy of Gurudwara Pathar Sahib still resonating within us. The prospect of exploring Leh and Ladakh on two wheels fueled our eagerness for the adventures that awaited us in the coming days.

As night fell, our group convened around the dinner table. Though the meal was satisfactory, tonight it left something to be desired. Nevertheless, our hunger prevailed, and we enjoyed a hearty dinner. Following the meal, Ankit and I ventured out to explore Leh city under the veil of night. The sky was adorned with clouds, and the moon took center stage, casting a gentle glow. The city, quiet and with most places closed, exuded a serene charm with only a handful of souls wandering about. Venturing a kilometer or two, we found no open shops but embraced the natural tranquility before returning to the hotel.

Later in the night, our group of 11 gathered in one room. Meenal suggested a card game initially, but its complexity discouraged everyone from delving into such mentally taxing gameplay. After a brief discussion, we settled on a more entertaining option—drumsradh. The game involved acting out a movie name while the rest of the group attempted to guess it. Meenal's team presented one of the least sound bollywood movie name "Albert Pinto Ko Gussa Kyun Nahi Aata." Even I wasn't familiar with the title, but it turned out to be a well-known film. Meenal faced the challenge of acting out the complex name, beginning with the letter "Albert."

Struggling to depict the scientist, she eventually resorted to a clever move, mimicking the inventor of the bulb. However, a teammate, Pratiek, promptly corrected her, noting that it was Thomas Edison, not Albert Einstein, who invented the bulb. The realization prompted laughter, and Meenal adjusted her strategy. She shifted to the first letter of "Ankit," and their team successfully conveyed "A." Through this clever wordplay, they ultimately arrived at "Albert." Although challenging, the unfamiliar movie title secured our victory.

The game continued with more movies, and the diverse group from around the country added to the enjoyment, especially in the unique setting of Leh at night. By the time the clock struck 2 am, we decided to call it a night. We headed to our respective rooms, set multiple alarms for the early morning departure at 9 am, and succumbed to a deep and restful sleep, a testament to the exhaustion from our adventurous day.

Ride towards Nubra Valley: *culture exposure*

यदा भवन्तः यात्रां कुर्वन्ति, तदा भवन्तः जीवनस्य यथार्थं अर्थं आविष्करोति

When you travel, you discover the true meaning of life

The following morning, I awoke naturally around 6:30 am, the absence of any alarm adding to the sense of calm. As I drew back the curtains, I was greeted by the early sun hovering just above the mountains, casting a warm glow over Leh city. The atmosphere was markedly different, a blend of anticipation and trepidation lingering within me, for today marked the beginning of my motorcycle journey through some of the highest motorable places on Earth.

Stepping outside onto the corridor, bathed in the morning sunlight, I indulged in a cup of tea, savoring the breathtaking panorama of Leh. The view encompassed snow-capped hills, vibrant greenery, and the tranquil city below. In the next half-hour, the rest of the group gradually stirred, and we collectively decided to reconvene for breakfast around 8:30.

Eager to embrace the day's adventure, I swiftly got ready and packed my belongings. Heading downstairs with Ankit, we performed a thorough test ride on our Himalayan bikes—a mixture of excitement and a hint of apprehension accompanying us. The bikes proved promising during the test ride, reinforcing our confidence for the journey ahead.

Returning for breakfast, I opted for a hearty meal, mindful that lunch might be scarce during our ride. The spread included parathas, milk, bread, omelets, and yogurt, providing the perfect fuel for the day. Following breakfast, we gathered our luggage and loaded it into the accompanying traveler, which would journey with us, accommodating six members of our group. The traveler's role extended beyond mere transportation; its driver was also tasked with guiding us along the route and ensuring our bikes' fuel and security needs were met.

The bike vendor was well-prepared, offering us all the necessary gear for our ride. They took the time to inform us about the details of the road ahead and the requirements for a safe journey. From helmets to gloves and maps, they ensured that we were equipped with everything we needed. Their thorough briefing instilled confidence in us, knowing that we were well-prepared for the adventure ahead. Equipped with all the necessary safety gear — knee guards, elbow guards, and scratched helmet(although bit smaller in size) — I took a moment to appreciate the added layers of protection. It was a novel experience, having such comprehensive security measures for a bike ride. It took the next half-hour for our entire group to be fully geared up for the day's ride.

Positioning my bike in front of our traveler, we gathered together, capturing the moment with numerous photos that marked the commencement of the day's journey. Our destination for the day was the Nubra Valley, a ride spanning approximately 170-190 kilometers and anticipated to take 6-8 hours, according to Tashi, our traveler driver.

With my body fully encased in protective gear, I set out on the bike ride, embracing the uncertainty that lay ahead.

The allure of the unknown was part of the thrill, and I

approached the journey with the mindset to savor and relish every moment. This, after all, was the essence of my trip to Leh — a retreat from urban clamor, a departure from crowds, and an immersion in nature to find solace.

As I ventured into the embrace of nature, I could feel its healing touch from within. Allowing the magic of nature to unfold, I embraced the journey with an open heart, ready to be captivated by the scenic wonders and find inner peace along the winding roads of Leh.

As I gradually accelerated through the city on my bike, a sense of anticipation and adventure enveloped me. The rhythmic hum of the engine resonated against the backdrop of Leh's landscape. Our group, dispersed across separate bikes, added to the diverse tableau of bikers traversing the city streets. Among us, Rohit, accompanied by his wife Snehal, shared the road as we embarked on this collective biking venture. Pratiek, the seasoned road warrior, and Ankit, the avid traveler, were both ready and eager to embark on the bike ride together.

The cold air, tinged with the crispness of high-altitude surroundings, permeated our journey. It was a sensation our bodies would need to grow accustomed to, considering the riding conditions we were set to encounter over the next few days. With unanimous agreement, we decided to ride in close formation, fostering a sense of unity as we ventured into the heart of Leh.

At the subsequent checkpoint, Tashi, our traveler driver, efficiently managed the necessary entries on our behalf. These periodic stops, peppered along our route, served as crucial gateways, ensuring our safe passage by regulating the impact of unpredictable weather conditions on our journey.

Leaving the urban landscape in our rearview mirrors, we embraced the natural wonders of valleys that unfolded before us. It felt as if nature itself extended a warm invitation, beckoning us into its pristine realm. The roads, generously broad, accommodated our formation as we rode side by side, carving through the twists and turns typical of valley terrain. Towering mountains surrounded us, creating a majestic panorama that only intensified as we ascended toward the zenith of the valleys, each bend revealing a fresh tableau of awe-inspiring beauty.

After nearly an hour of riding, I noticed our traveler had come to a halt at a captivating viewpoint in Leh. As each of us on our bikes arrived one by one, we dismounted, relishing the chance to stretch our legs and take in the surroundings. The transition from city riding to the valleys was palpable, with a noticeable drop in temperature. The cold wind brushed against us, a stark contrast to the more sheltered city streets.

Standing at the cliff's edge, I gazed ahead, greeted by a breathtaking natural panorama that unfolded like a living painting. The mountains, both grand and intimate valleys, and the snow-capped peaks discreetly peeking from behind the rugged terrain formed a stunning tableau. It became apparent why these mountains were devoid of trees; the relentless wind, low moisture, and frigid temperatures created an environment inhospitable to much vegetation. In awe of the spectacle, we captured the moment through pictures, savoring the first stop on our bike journey, blissfully unaware of the thrilling and challenging adventure that awaited us at our next destination: KhardungLa.

Tashi's call prompted us to kick-start our engines early, as the journey to Nubra Valley promised to be a long one. I mounted my bike, inhaling deeply as excitement mingled with the anticipation of the scenic routes that lay ahead. The next 30 minutes saw me reaching another checkpoint where Tashi awaited us. After the necessary check-in procedures, we embarked on the ascent to KhardungLa, one of the highest peaks on our itinerary.

As I navigated through the mesmerizing landscape, every twist and turn brought about a change in scenery. The journey began with a light drizzle, transforming into our first encounter with snowfall within 5-10 minutes. Riding through the snow on a decent road, flanked by naked mountains behind, partially snow-capped ones en route, and fully snow-clad peaks ahead, I was enraptured by the beauty of nature.

Around 11:30 am, our group paused by the roadside. Stepping into the unexpected snowfall, I reveled in the spontaneous joy shared with fellow travelers. Although unprepared for such wintry conditions, my jacket proved to be a reliable shield against the cold. We lingered, adapting to the sudden temperature drop and the snow-laden environment. Restarting my bike, I set it in first gear, phone in hand, capturing the extraordinary moments of my inaugural road trip to the highest motorable pass amidst the snow.

Five minutes later, numbness set into my hands, prompting a brief stop to glove up and shield against the cold. As I continued the ascent, I witnessed the transformation of once-naked mountains into snow-covered wonders, the temperature plummeting, and the biting wind intensifying the chill. On one side, a colossal mountain soared, while on the other, a steep snow-covered descent awaited.

After an hour of traversing this breathtaking terrain, I finally spotted a gathering of vans and bikes. Reaching the apex of KhardungLa pass, I parked my bike beside my trip companions, feeling a sense of achievement and elation. The snowy surroundings added a unique charm, especially for those encountering snow for the first time outside the city.

Amidst colorful prayer flags fluttering in the brisk mountain air, we stood at the pinnacle, 18,938 feet above sea level, capturing the moment with a group photo beside the sign marking our presence at the top. This experience reinforced the idea that nature is a source of freshness, calmness, and countless other sensations. The flags, often used in Buddhism pilgrimages, added a positive aura to the environment.

We lingered briefly at the summit until Tashi urged us to depart early, emphasizing the need to clear the upcoming checkpoint before the potential intensification of snowfall. Police regulations mandated chains on wheels for snow-covered roads, and further snowfall could lead to restrictions on the route. Grasping the memory of KhardungLa in my heart, I descended from the peak with a profound appreciation for nature's beauty, calmness, and the potential dangers that coexist in this extraordinary realm.

Descending from the KhardungLa pass, the weather improved, revealing clear views of the spectacular snow-capped mountains that surrounded me. About 15-20 minutes into the descent, I decided to pull over and soak in the awe-inspiring scenery. Ankit, riding behind me, joined in, and we found ourselves immersed in conversation about the sheer excitement and beauty of the last few days, a dream trip unfolding far from the familiar landscapes of Hyderabad.

Amidst the mesmeric setting, Ankit finally acknowledged that I had brought him to Leh—a dream we had nurtured since our college days. The cold wind, once biting, now felt invigorating. Resuming our bike journey, we still had 10-15 kilometers to cover before reaching the next checkpoint where Tashi, our traveler driver, awaited us. A hint of hunger spurred me onward as I navigated the downhill stretch in the marvelous surroundings.

Each passing second etched memories in my mind, attempting to encapsulate the calm, smooth, stable, and natural essence of the journey. Riding side by side, Ankit and I shouted in unison from our bikes, adding a bit of noise to the surreal experience. The bike's speed increased as we descended, creating an exhilarating sensation. After nearly an hour of traversing through what felt like heaven on Earth, I reached the downhill checkpoint, Northpullu.

The checkpoint bustled with fellow travelers taking a break, enjoying tea and food. Our group patiently waited, and I parked my bike before freshening up in the hotel's washroom. Behind the hotels, yaks grazed peacefully against the backdrop of rocky, snow-capped mountains.

I ordered coffee and indulged in "*pahado wali maggi*" for lunch—a mountain-themed delight. Some members of our group, fatigued by the twists and turns of the mountainous road, rested on chairs, heads tilted back for relief. The sun added a touch of warmth, creating a comforting atmosphere. Venturing to the back of the hotel with Ankit, we marveled at the yaks and the majestic mountains. Capturing these moments through photographs, I gazed upwards, realizing that we had conquered the summit of KhardungLa pass on our bikes—an unforgettable ride etched in memory.

As our coffee and maggi arrived, the unexpected taste in this setting made the meal particularly satisfying. With two rounds of coffee and maggi, I replenished my energy reserves for the road ahead toward Nubra valley. Around 2 PM, we set out from Northpullu towards Spituk, following Tashi's directive to meet at Diskit—a destination that lay approximately 2-3 hours of driving away from the Northpullu checkpoint.

As I maneuvered through the sinuous roads, my one-handed filming escapade added an extra layer of exhilaration to the journey. The dynamic landscape underwent a captivating metamorphosis, unfolding into a rugged expanse of rocky mountains. Towering peaks surrounded me, occasionally punctuated by the rhythmic sounds of rocks being chiseled by dedicated laborers, fortifying the paths against potential rockfalls.

Traversing the challenging rocky terrain for next an hour, I chanced upon a stretch of pristine, straight road—a stark contrast to the preceding ruggedness. A congregation of bikers had congregated at a strategic point, and I seamlessly joined the line, parking my bike alongside Ankit and our fellow riders. The collective aura among the bikers was charged with anticipation. Taking a moment to absorb the surroundings, I perched on a roadside rock, immersing myself in the splendor of the rocky mountains and the meandering river that carved through the valleys—a scene so spectacular it resembled an untouched canvas awaiting the stroke of an artist's brush.

As I reveled in the breathtaking panorama, I seized the moment to capture solo pictures amidst the camaraderie of fellow bikers. We lingered in that scenic haven, allowing the tranquility to wash over us, before setting out on the next leg of our adventure, destined for Diskit Monastery—our rendezvous point with Tashi. The sheer joy of the ride intensified, the throttle of the bike synchronizing seamlessly with the captivating beauty of the environment, creating a harmonious fusion of thrill and natural splendor that fueled the spirit of our journey. After next an hour of driving, around 4 pm, I arrived at a crucial turning point. This junction presented two divergent paths—one leading towards Siachen, the highest point, and the other guiding us to our intended destination, Diskit. Patiently waiting at the crossroads for the rest of the group on bikes, Ankit soon joined me, and together, we set our course for Diskit.

Once again, my bike surged ahead, and within the next half-hour, I found myself at the river point. It was a breathtaking sight—the supposed Indus River meandering through the landscape, adorned with small rocks, pristine water flowing gracefully, and encircled by majestic mountains. As the clock approached 4:30 pm, a Go-karting facility came into view, signaling that Diskit was approximately 10 km away. Our traveler vehicle was parked nearby, and our exuberant group eagerly awaited our arrival.

I parked my bike adjacent to the go-karting spot, which boasted ample parking space. The prospect of adventure activities like go-karting and ATV driving in the valleys was tempting. Despite the allure, our group of bikers, well-acquainted with the thrill of navigating the challenging terrains on our motorcycles, collectively opted out of go-karting. We understood that what we were experiencing on our bikes far surpassed the adventure offered by these recreational activities. Hence, we politely declined the invitation to engage in go-karting, choosing to revel in the unmatched excitement of our two-wheeled journey through the dramatic landscapes.

Despite the journey's unexpected turns, hunger struck, and fortunately, food options were at our disposal. Ankit and I indulged in a feast, savoring the delectable combination of Chhole samosa, maggi, and tea. The samosa, in particular, stood out as one of the best I had ever tasted. Perhaps it was the unique charm of the place, the intensity of our hunger, or the sheer delight of stumbling upon such unexpected culinary delights in an equally unexpected location that made the experience truly memorable.

Positioning myself beside the go-kart track, I settled into a chair, allowing my thoughts to unfold over the next half-hour. Contemplating the essence of nature, I found myself pondering the undue pressures, issues, work-related stresses, familial concerns, and the uncertainties of the future that we all carry. In that moment, a realization crystallized: amidst the complexities of life, the ultimate solution lies in aligning with one's nature. It dawned on me that the only impediment to our pursuits is often self-imposed.

Life, I mused, is inherently challenging, and if it feels too facile, it likely means we're not pushing our boundaries. Embracing the beauty of nature, I sensed that it holds the key to navigating life's various terrains. By embracing the natural course of things, one can overcome any obstacle. It became clear that we are the architects of our limitations; only we can thwart our progress.

With this newfound perspective, I ceased overthinking and allowed my gaze to wander. The surroundings, a testament to nature's ceaseless ability to astonish and educate simultaneously, captivated my senses. This solitary interlude in a remarkable place became a profound experience—a communion with myself and the natural world that left an indelible imprint on my soul.

My group beckoned me just as they were gearing up for their go-kart adventure. Eager to document their thrilling escapade, I meticulously captured videos and pictures, tracing their every move around the track. It turned out to be a delightful time spent near the go-karting point.

Around 5:40 pm, we decided to set forth as Diskit Monastery was slated to close by 6 pm. The route towards the monastery presented a straight road, flanked by expansive open spaces on both sides. Seizing the opportunity, I pushed my bike to its peak speed of 100+, relishing the exhilarating ride along the straight stretch. In a mere 15 minutes of blissful biking, we arrived at Diskit Monastery.

Diskit Monastery, an ancient and grand structure in Diskit, boasted an imposing 100-foot-tall statue of Lord Buddha. Stepping inside, we were enveloped by an awe-inspiring atmosphere, as the sculptures and portraits that adorned the monastery dated back to the 14th century. Buddhist priests engaged in their daily prayers added to the spiritual ambiance. The expansive lobby surrounding the Buddha statue provided a serene space for reflection.

Diskit Monastery

From the monastery's vantage point, Diskit village unfolded in all its charm, nestled amidst river and mountains. The view extended to the vast Nubra Valley, a sprawling desert that beckoned as our next destination. Spending almost half an hour absorbing the cultural richness and panoramic vistas, we captured the moment before descending to where our traveler and bikes were parked.

With a sense of camaraderie, the girls in our group ascended above the traveler, and together we immortalized the epic moment with a group photo. Without lingering, we promptly mounted our bikes and set off towards Nubra Valley, eager to explore the enchanting white desert and encounter the distinctive charm of camels in that breathtaking landscape. Embarking on the next leg of our journey, I eased into the changing roads and surroundings, gradually sensing a shift in the atmosphere. Before me, it was stretched a vast expanse of a pristine white desert. Overwhelmed by the stark contrast between the rocky terrain and the sandy landscape, I pulled over to the side, taking a few moments to etch the distinctive scenery into both my memory and camera.

In approximately 20 minutes, we reached the vicinity of the desert, specifically the Kayak Road in Hunder. Parking my bike beside the river that had accompanied us on our journey, I marveled at the sight of dozens of camels leisurely scattered about, surrounded by the white desert, a flowing river, and towering rocky mountains—an awe-inspiring tableau of nature.

While some of our group members ventured towards camel rides, I opted to sit at the edge of the river, captivated by the soothing flow of water, the expansive desert, and the majestic mountains. Time seemed to stand still as we immersed ourselves in this breathtaking landscape, spending nearly half an hour before setting off for our overnight stay in Nubra Valley.

It was then that fellow travelers, revealed that it was Dhanshree's daughter's birthday, and plans for a celebration were afoot. The group of bikers forged ahead in search of a special surprise for Dhanshree, our fellow traveler, without giving away the secret. Our mission was to find a cake for a memorable celebration at our overnight stop. Despite our best efforts, we couldn't locate a bakery along the way. One shop we found was closed at the time, adding a sense of adventure to our journey. Undeterred, we continued on our path, determined to make the most of our evening. The anticipation of the surprise and the camaraderie among us made the ride all the more exciting.

Our accommodations, a beautiful cottage nestled in the heart of the valley, greeted us within the next 10-15 minutes. The rooms exuded a sense of living amidst the embracing valleys.

We discussed our concern with our driver. Tashi, being a local of Nubra Valley, offered to help find a cake. I accompanied him on a quest that led us to a nearby bakery. Alongside the cake, I couldn't resist picking up some local cookies that looked both delicious and tempting. Returning to our cottage hotel, we stowed the cake in my room, concealing it to preserve the element of surprise.

Sharing a room with Ankit, we marveled at its uniqueness and cleanliness. However, the mystery of the source of the draft eluded us. To prepare for the night, Ankit left the tap open, per the hotel's instructions, anticipating hot water. To our surprise, the wait extended to at least half an hour. Eventually, warmth graced us, and after freshening up and changing into clean attire, I found solace sitting outside my room, reflecting on the unparalleled experience of navigating the top roads in India—a moment both amazing and priceless.

As I reminisced, Meenal emerged from her room, and we gathered with the rest of the group who were staying in adjacent rooms. She shared the unexpected news of a power cut around 11 pm. Undeterred, we convened for dinner around 9 pm. The hunger from a day of travel with no proper lunch made the hearty spread of soups, chapati, curries, and desserts taste like a culinary perfection. The evening was spent relishing the delicious fare and engaging in animated discussions about our trip, the events, and the places we had encountered. The collective excitement and joy mirrored my own, creating an atmosphere of camaraderie and contentment.

After relishing dinner for half an hour, I handed the key to Ankit, entrusting him with the task of bringing in the birthday cake for Dhanshree's daughter. Eager to witness the joyous surprise unfold, I envisioned the delight in Dhanshree's eyes as she discovered our thoughtful gesture. The day had been a bit somber for her, missing her daughter on her birthday.

As the cake graced the table, Dhanshree's sister, Swaralee, led her to the celebration. Dhanshree, sporting a radiant smile and attempting to contain her happy tears, instantly brightened. Overwhelmed with joy, she promptly called her daughter, bringing them together via video call. We collectively reveled in the celebration, savoring the cake and each joyous moment. By now, the clock had struck 10 pm.

With the cake enjoyed, Meenal retrieved her UNO cards, sparking a new wave of amusement. Gathering around the table, we delved into the game just as the clock ticked toward the imminent power outage at 11 pm. Undeterred, we played UNO with boisterous laughter and good-natured cheating, creating an atmosphere that must have left onlookers wondering when the power cut would finally occur.

In an effort to include the workers in our celebration, we shared a slice of cake with them, and they arranged a few candles. Our UNO session continued unabated for the next hour, featuring an abundance of 4+ and 2+ cards that prolonged the game, as UNO games are wont to do. True to form, the game persisted even as the power cut happened around 11:20 pm. Slowly, we dispersed to our respective rooms, bidding farewell to the lively scene at the Nubra Valley. The night unfolded in the soft glow of moonlight, with mountains framing the vista and an air of tranquility enveloping the surroundings—an indescribable beauty that could only be felt.

Taking in the mesmerizing ambiance for a while, I eventually retired to my room, knowing that the next day would bring another day of early departure and the promise of a challenging and adventurous journey towards Pangong Lake, according to Tashi's route.

Finally, The Pangong Lake: Multi-Weather ride

जीवनं भव्यं साहसिकं वा किमपि नास्ति वा
Life is either a grand adventure or nothing

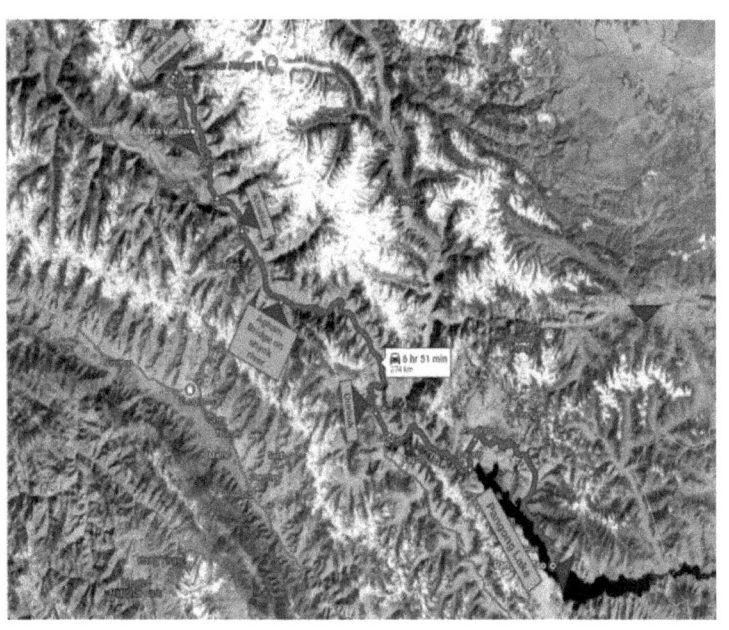

The tranquility of my final night's sleep in Nubra Valley bestowed a deep and restful slumber, leaving me remarkably refreshed the next morning. Rising early, around 5-6 AM, I ventured out of the cottage into the crisp morning air. The invigorating cold and the pristine sight of the mountains greeted me, sending a thrill through my body. My first stop was the canteen, where a steaming cup of coffee awaited me. Carrying my warm beverage, I strolled into the garden, where the panoramic view unfolded before me—clear and breathtaking.

Seated amidst nature's grandeur, I spent nearly an hour in contemplation. The quietude allowed my mind to sift through various thoughts, finding clarity and solutions. It dawned on me that nature, in all its simplicity, is the ultimate truth, and our mental disturbances are often self-imposed. The serenity of that environment left an indelible impression.

Soon, Meenal, Tapasya, and Sakshi joined me in the garden. We relished tea together and engaged in discussions about the day's upcoming journey. After a leisurely time outdoors, I returned to my room, while they captured the beautiful morning surroundings in photographs. Anticipating an early delivery of hot water, I had requested it earlier, and true to expectation, it arrived promptly. A refreshing shower left me energized for the day ahead, although I remained unaware of the challenges that lay in wait during our journey.

Gathering at the canteen around 8:30 AM, we were treated to a delicious and nutritious breakfast. Anticipating a lack of lunch options on the way to Pangong, I opted for an extra helping, ensuring sustenance for the day's adventure. Little did I know what twists and turns awaited us in the unfolding journey.

The pivotal moment arrived, and with a surge of excitement, I kick-started my bike, leading the way ahead of our traveler van. As I navigated around the Nubra Valley, the small yet incredibly beautiful city resonated with a sense of proximity to nature. Beyond the valley, the road stretched out into a straight path for the next few kilometers. Eager to capture the essence of the journey, I recorded videos and accelerated my bike to speeds exceeding 100, reveling in the expansive plains flanked by towering valleys and mountains on both sides for next half an hour. This particular stretch of road was one of the longest and straightest I had encountered on our trip. As Snehal sat behind Rohit on the bike, she skillfully captured some of our best moments on video. The wide, smooth road and the stunning scenery provided the perfect backdrop for our adventure. I had a feeling that these videos would become some of the most cherished memories of our journey. For the next half an hour, I relished every moment of the ride, soaking in the beauty of the surroundings and the joy of being on the road with my fellow bikers. The wind in my hair and the freedom of the open road filled me with a sense of exhilaration that I knew would stay with me long after the trip was over.

Reaching village near Taksha, the first checkpoint on our way to Pangong Lake, I parked by the roadside. It was a familiar spot, having passed through it the previous day on our journey to Nubra. Here, the road diverged—one direction leading to Pangong Lake, our destination for the day, and another signposted for Siachen, a stark reminder of the harsh realities faced by those stationed in the world's highest battlefield. The weather was remarkably pleasant, with a gentle breeze replacing the biting cold of the previous days.

After a brief 10-minute pause, the rest of the trip companions arrived. To our collective astonishment, Pratiek, one of our avid bikers, revealed that Snehal had misplaced her mobile phone along the way. The news struck a chord of concern, considering she had been seated behind Rohit, capturing videos of our journey. Despite the gravity of the situation, addressing it had to be deferred, as she was visibly upset. The chances of getting phone back was very low, since there were no network available in the mobile.

While Pratiek and Rohit scoured the roadside in an attempt to locate the phone, the rest of us found ourselves at the road junction, idling away the time by capturing photos on our bikes and engaging in lighthearted antics. The rest of us, filled with a sense of freedom and joy, decided to make the most of the moment. We danced in the middle of the road, our movements fluid and uninhibited. Some of us climbed on nearby structures, playfully mimicking monkeys, and explored the surroundings with a childlike curiosity. Laughter filled the air as we embraced the carefree spirit of the moment, letting go of any worries or stress. It was a lighthearted and memorable experience, one that reminded us to cherish the simple joys in life. It dawned on me that these seemingly trivial moments of childlike enjoyment were what we often overlooked in our routine lives, and rediscovering that sense of playfulness infused a surge of energy.

As the search for the lost phone proved futile, we collectively decided to resume our journey to the next destination. Late as it was, I restarted my bike, following the others. Tashi, our traveler driver, skillfully navigated the challenging road ahead. However, within the next half-hour, I lost sight of the traveler, leaving me to traverse the winding roads independently.

For the subsequent half-hour, the initial winding roads ascended to the top of the valley, only to descend sharply to the other side. Finding myself at the valley's bottom marked a drastic change in the road and the surroundings. The rocky terrain, strewn with small stones, posed a formidable challenge, and multiple diversions further complicated the path. Thoughts of losing my way crossed my mind numerous times, but the natural beauty enveloping me—dust swirling, stones scattered across the road, and towering mountains on the horizon—crafted a mesmerizing backdrop.

After driving for another half-hour, I spotted Ankit and Pratiek standing by the roadside, an indication that we had collectively veered off course. Parking my bike beside theirs, we sat for a while, engaged in discussions about the nature and environment surrounding us. Despite capturing a beautiful panorama, the road conditions were not conducive to an enjoyable bike ride.

Reaffirming our commitment to the chosen path, I led the way ahead. The landscape now featured ongoing construction work. Negotiating the rocky path and construction zones for the next half-hour, I glimpsed a village in the distance. As I reached the spot, I found our friends already there, taking a break. It was the near Khalsar, spanning a river below and surrounded by a cluster of shops.

With an appetite for a quick snack, we replenish our energy. Some of the fellow travelers on the van were experiencing dizziness from the twisting valley roads and the dusty trail. Seeking a moment of tranquility, I descended to the bridge, perching on a stone in the center of the river. The view was serene, the river cascading from the heights above and flowing beneath the bridge—a natural beauty to savor. Ankit and Pratiek joined me, and we indulged in puffs and tea, embracing the peaceful ambiance.

The weather hinted at a change, prompting Tashi, our guide, to suggest an early departure. As we prepared to continue our journey, the sense of camaraderie and the awe-inspiring landscapes hinted at the adventure that awaited us on the road to Pangong Lake.

I revved up my bike, embarking on the route towards Durbuk. After covering 2-3 km, my vision was obscured by a blanket of dust, whipped up by relentless winds that threatened to carry me away. The stony road became enveloped in a haze, prompting me to halt. Glancing back, I noticed Ankit, similarly halted on his bike. When the wind subsided, we cautiously resumed our journey through the dusty terrain, strewn with stones.

As the road straightened, the terrain improved, revealing a landscape that resembled an extraterrestrial planet. After nearly half an hour, I reached the pinnacle of the valleys, where the scenery underwent a dramatic transformation. Pausing with Pratiek, we marveled at the breathtaking view, reminiscent of what one might envision as a "death valley." The roads hugged the valleys closely, offering a surreal experience as I navigated within arm's reach of the cliffs. On one side, a series of valleys unfolded, while on the other, a steep drop created an intense sense of peril. Despite the apparent danger, the exhilaration of driving through this desolate and untamed landscape was unparalleled. The absence of any signs of human habitation added to the mystique, making it feel like a forbidden, no-man's-land.

The adventure continued for the next half-hour as we drove through this Death Valley, the vastness of the surroundings evoking a sense of awe. Spotting Ankit waiting ahead on the side of the road marked a change in scenery—a straight

road lay ahead, with a river crossing in sight. Shiny stones of varying sizes adorned the road, mirroring the riverbed's composition. As anticipated, rain began to fall, starting slowly and escalating into a heavy downpour within minutes. Undeterred, Ankit, Pratiek, and I decided to embrace the rain, continuing our bike ride rather than seeking shelter. As we continued on our journey, we came across the Agham Bridge route, which spanned the Shyok River, famously known as the "River of Death." Despite its ominous name, the area was incredibly serene, with no signs of human presence, only the quiet beauty of nature surrounding us. The stillness of the surroundings added to the awe-inspiring atmosphere, making us feel like we were truly in the midst of untouched wilderness.

As we ventured further, we encountered several challenges typical of such remote and rugged terrain. River crossings, sections affected by landslides, and rough, pitched roads tested our riding skills and endurance. However, each obstacle we overcame added to the satisfaction of the ride. The breathtaking environment, with its stark beauty and raw wilderness, made every challenge worth it, creating a memorable and rewarding experience for all of us.

The raindrops infiltrated my helmet, but the jacket provided a shield against the intrusion. The surroundings transformed into a spectacle—rainfall, a sprawling river, small valleys, and the encircling mountains. The cold wind intensified as the road inclined along the valley. Riding at a steady speed, my focus narrowed on navigating through the stones. The risk of skidding loomed, particularly in the rain and riverbank conditions, which gradually turned the road muddy. Nonetheless, it was an enthralling experience, a harmonious blend of weather, environment, and challenging road conditions.

After an hour of traversing this dynamic landscape, I finally reached the summit of the valleys near Durbuk. There, I found Rohit patiently waiting for us in a makeshift shelter resembling a small restaurant. Parking my bike alongside Pratiek and Ankit, we sought refuge from the rain, feeling a mix of relief and exhilaration after the adventurous drive through muddy and stony roads. Inside the shelter, we indulged in piping hot tea, savoring the warmth it provided.

As I tried to reach Tashi for an update on their location, I noticed the frustrating absence of a mobile network. Despite our best efforts, we were unable to establish a connection, leaving us in the dark about their whereabouts. Undeterred, we decided to continue our journey after a brief 30-minute break with a coffee. The delay gave us a chance to rest and regroup, but the uncertainty of not being able to reach Tashi lingered in the back of our minds. Nevertheless, we remained optimistic and determined to enjoy the rest of our ride, hoping to reconnect with them soon.

Just 1 km ahead, we encountered Tashi waiting for us. They had reached half an hour earlier but were unaware of our proximity due to the lack of mobile network coverage. Sharing stories of our journey, we relished the scenic beauty, discussed the challenges of navigating through stones, rivers, and heavy rain. Taking a moment to enjoy some snacks in the traveler, we warmed ourselves before setting out again toward Durbuk, our eyes set on reaching Pangong by evening.

After a drive of approximately 15-20 minutes, we reached the next petrol pump in Durbuk. Eager to ensure our bikes were topped up with fuel, we made a pit stop and basked in the welcome warmth of sunlight. The rain had subsided, unveiling a sunny day ahead. Tashi informed us that it would take about 2-3 hours to reach Pangong from this point.

Some fellow travelers on the van were grappling with feelings of dizziness and nausea—common symptoms for those unaccustomed to navigating the twisting valley roads. Chaitanya, seeking respite from the motion sickness, inquired if she could join us on bikes to Pangong. Recognizing the distraction that the scenic surroundings provided, she hopped onto a bike.

Embarking from the petrol pump, I gradually accelerated, noting the changing landscape as we approached Pangong. The roads widened, the mountains accumulated more dust, and construction work signaled potential changes to this adventurous route in the coming years. The twists and turns persisted for the next hour until we were promised a glimpse of the replica of Phugal Valley along the way.

Around 5:30 pm, after another half-hour of riding, one side of the road transformed into a wide-ranging scene of greenery. Distant yaks and sheep grazed above the mountains, and I parked my bike at the roadside. The sight of Phugal replicas, with grass forming spherical chunks, created a unique and mesmerizing field of greenery. Bikers and I took a break, soaking in the unconventional beauty

and capturing the scenes. As Tashi was set to meet us directly at Pangong Lake, and time was running late, we decided to continue our journey and stop at Pangong.

Maintaining a constant speed on the stone-laden roads, I marveled at the unfolding scenery. Around 6:15 pm, a colossal lake came into view. Its enormity left me awestruck—open fields on one side, mountains adorning the other, and clouds reflecting vividly in the calm waters. Never before had I witnessed such a vast and serene lake surrounded by such breathtaking beauty. I parked my bike by the side, captivated by the spectacle.

After a brief pause, I resumed my ride, anticipating that others had reached Pangong and were awaiting my arrival to check in. Spotting Tashi descending towards the lake, I followed suit, taking a left for our overnight stay in one of the camps. Meeting fellow bikers just a kilometer ahead, we made a U-turn to descend towards Pangong Lake. In a matter of minutes, we were in close proximity to our lodging. With plans to freshen up briefly and enjoy tea, we looked forward to savoring the enchanting allure of Pangong Lake.

Upon entering my room, I arranged my luggage and took a moment to rest. Ankit burst in with somewhat unsettling news—there was no hot water available in the frigid temperature, and the area had no mobile network signal. The cold, hovering around 1-2 degrees, was intensified by a biting wind. Nevertheless, after a brisk freshening up, I headed to the dining area. A cup of tea became my refuge from the chilly conditions. Within the next 15 minutes, we all congregated, sipped tea, and set off for Pangong Lake in the traveler. The lake was a mere 100-200 meters from our abode, and the final leg required a chilly walk.

In the late evening, the cold was palpable as we approached the famed Pangong Lake. Situated at almost 14,000 feet above sea level, with only a third of its expanse in India and the rest in China, the lake's tranquility mirrored the clouds reflecting on its serene waters. Beyond the lake stretched beautiful, towering mountains. The climate and scenery coalesced into an unparalleled portrait of natural beauty. Pangong Lake's cinematic allure had graced several Bollywood movies, such as "3 Idiots" and "Jab Tak Hai Jaan." Vendors recreated iconic scenes from these films, offering props for visitors to immerse themselves in the cinematic experience. One vendor event sold cricket equipment, inviting spontaneous games by the lake. Playing cricket in such an environment marked one of the trip's most memorable moments.

Tapasya, our avid dream traveller, fulfilled a lifelong wish of capturing herself at Pangong Lake in a saree. Each traveler reveled in their hard-earned moments, relishing the adventure that had brought them to this breathtaking destination. After spending more time by the lake, we returned to our camps. I made a mental note to return early the next morning to witness the sunrise— an enchanting experience amidst nature's wonders.

Back at the dining hall, we eagerly awaited dinner, which commenced around 8 PM. I started with a flavorful soup, savoring two more cups. The vegetarian dinner, though non-vegetarian options were available, surpassed expectations, possibly heightened by the day's adventures and lingering hunger. As we wrapped up our meal, we lingered in the dining hall, engaging in discussions about our journey. A member of the staff played music, and soon, we found ourselves dancing. The cold surroundings at Pangong Lake inspired the invention of the "*Kambal Dance,*" a playful and amusing dance born out of necessity. Despite the chilly temperatures, Pratiek was reluctant to emerge from his warm kambal (blanket), but he was eventually persuaded to join in the dance.

As we began to dance, our energy and enthusiasm attracted the attention of other travelers and staff nearby. Before long, they joined us in the impromptu dance, creating a lively and joyful atmosphere. The moment was captured in photos and videos, immortalizing the spontaneous and fun-filled memory at Pangong Lake.

Aware of the impending power cut at 11 PM, a déjà vu from Nubra Valley, we enjoyed the lively atmosphere until the lights went out precisely at 11 PM. Stepping outside, I gazed at the sky—cloudy yet clear—and marveled at the proximity of the moon. The night sky at Pangong Lake offered a mesmerizing view of the stars, with multiple galaxies visible in the vast expanse above. The clarity of the sky was remarkable, allowing us to see celestial bodies with stunning detail.

Gazing up at the heavens, it felt as though we were being transported to another realm, far away from the cares of the world. The beauty and majesty of the night sky were so captivating that one could easily lose themselves in the wonder of it all. It was a moment of pure magic, a reminder of the vastness and mystery of the universe.

Contemplating the prospect of the morning sunrise, fueled by this sense of wonder, I retired for the night. Wrapped in the chilly embrace of my blanket, the anticipation of the morning sunrise over the mountains and the vast lake played on my mind throughout the night. Amid thoughts of the trip, the tranquility of life, and the serenity enveloping me, I drifted into sleep, unaware of the passing time. The jarring sound of my alarm at 6 AM abruptly brought me back to consciousness. Despite the incomplete slumber, I hurriedly rose, freshened up in minutes, and dashed towards the door. As I opened it, a sight greeted me—snowflakes dancing in the sky. The entire scene had transformed overnight. While slightly disappointed that my expectation of a brilliant sunrise had shifted, I found solace and joy in capturing the enchanting change that had taken place. The mountains were now adorned with a fresh coat of snow, their reflections mirrored in the expansive lake. My bike and our camp homes were dusted with a layer of snow, and the mountains in the backdrop stood majestically under their snowy blankets. The ongoing snowfall, seemingly a dreamy touch, added a surreal quality to the morning.

Standing in the open, I immersed myself in the moment, forgetting about the biting cold. After a while, I made my way to the dining hall, where Tashi had spent the night. Sipping on a cup of tea, I relished the wintry ambiance. Tashi shared the news that a few girls in our group had fallen ill due to low oxygen levels. Meenal joined us, recounting how her roommates had experienced dizziness and vomiting throughout the night. Tashi had provided them with oxygen from the cylinder carried in the traveler, stabilizing their oxygen levels after about half an hour. Relieved, they joined

Snowcapped mountains around Pangong Lake

us in the dining hall, partaking in a modest breakfast. Feeling reassured about their well-being, I inquired about hot water for a bath. The caretaker informed me that people typically refrained from bathing for days, suggesting I skip it for the day. Nevertheless, he arranged a bucket of hot water, allowing me to freshen up and indulge in a quick, makeshift bath. Breakfast comprised poori sabji, bread, and coffee, savored against the backdrop of lingering snowfall outside.

With the weather still presenting a snowy spectacle, Tashi proposed a delay in our departure by an hour. Our destination was ChangLa pass, the highest motorable cliff in the mountains, and we aimed to reach the Leh district by day's end. Given the weather conditions, the checkpost would not permit travel towards the summit, prompting us to wait for clearer skies. We decided to set out after half an hour, keeping the distance and weather considerations in mind. During this time, we seized the opportunity to capture numerous photos, etching the ultimate trip into our memories. By now, our friends who had been unwell earlier were visibly improved, embracing the snowy morning tinged with gentle sunlight.

Adventurous ride to remember: Chang-LA Pass with heavy snowfall

अनिश्चिततायाः सम्मुखे अचञ्चलतया स्थित्वा साहसेन तस्य सम्मुखी भवन्तु

When faced with uncertainty, stand unwavering and confront it boldly

By 10 AM, I was fully geared up, my body shielded by a sturdy jacket, knees and elbows guarded, and my bike cleaned and set aside to soak up some warmth. Despite my helmet being a tad snug, providing a less-than-ideal fit for my face, it marked the final day of our journey to Leh. The bike vendor hadn't offered any alternatives, so I had managed to make do until now. Before embarking on the day's trip, I took one last sip of tea, savoring the moment in this incredible location surrounded by an amazing group of people.

Tashi led the way towards ChangLa pass, one of the highest motorable roads reaching remarkable altitudes. With snowfall and challenging road conditions ahead, Tashi advised extra caution. Our route would take us to the summit of ChangLa pass at nearly 18-19,000 feet, followed by a descent on the other side of the mountain. The entire stretch of road was expected to be challenging. The weather was poised to be a significant factor in today's journey. Despite the potential hurdles, I started with a positive mindset, intending to drive cautiously, especially during the ascent.

As I bid farewell to the Pangong lake, the surroundings unfolded before me in a series of breathtaking scenes. The transition from evening to morning had painted the landscape with an indescribable and mesmerizing beauty. The Pangong lake, adorned by the changing play of sunlight on the mountains, with and without snow, created an enchanting panorama that lingered in my memory.

In the next 15 minutes, I bid farewell to the mesmerizing Pangong lake and set my course towards Durbuk. In my contemplation, the enchanting beauty of Pangong Lake continued to weave its way into my thoughts. The road ahead was rugged, strewn with stones, and undergoing construction. For the next hour, we traversed this challenging terrain, driving through dusty valleys surrounded by majestic mountains. I maintained a controlled speed of 50-60 km/h, navigating the wide yet unpolished road. Despite the chilly atmosphere, the remnants of snow-capped peaks both behind and ahead of us added to the raw beauty of the surroundings.

Our rendezvous point with Tashi awaited us in Durbuk before we embarked on the ascent to the formidable ChangLa pass. In Durbuk, a crucial checkpoint was supposed to mark our entry, where we needed to obtain the necessary permits to traverse the towering mountain ahead. This checkpoint served a pivotal role, monitoring the movement of all vehicles ascending or descending, allowing for traffic regulation in response to the unpredictable weather conditions. These checkpoints used to be there beneath each high mountain.

After an hour, we arrived at Durbuk, all of us bikers driving together along this straight and expansive route. We halted near a restaurant, where I parked my bike and, to my surprise, discovered that the network had been restored after nearly a day of being unreachable. Ankit took the opportunity to call home and inform them about the temporary communication blackout. I also seized the moment to connect with my family. After some time, Tashi joined us at the restaurant, advising us to proceed to the checkpost. He cautioned that the entry might close soon, restricting further ascent into the ChangLa Pass mountains.

Resuming our journey, I ascended the mountain, feeling the temperature drop and spotting snow-capped peaks ahead.

Rainfall greeted us after 15 minutes, but undeterred, we continued our ascent on the bikes. Within the next half-hour, we reached the checkpost where Tashi awaited us. The rain had left my pants slightly damp, and as we waited for Tashi to secure the necessary permits, the cold wind intensified.

Tashi initiated the journey with the traveler and instructed us to rendezvous at the summit of ChangLa Pass, the pinnacle of the mountain. The ascent began alongside my fellow riders, with the rain intensifying. Despite the rain, the snow-capped mountains emerged into view, adding a captivating contrast to the landscape. The road gradually narrowed, winding through a series of turns. On this precarious path, vehicles descended rapidly, demanding heightened caution, particularly during turns. I maneuvered through the challenging terrain in second gear, maintaining a vigilant gaze on the road ahead.

The road conditions were the most treacherous encountered thus far, riddled with numerous potholes filled with water, making it challenging to distinguish between the road and the depressions. As I ascended, colossal rocks adorned with snow flanked the roadside, and the rain transitioned into a delicate snowfall, transforming the landscape into a hazardous yet enchanting panorama.

Suddenly, on a sharp turn, two vehicles descended rapidly, with the trailing vehicle seemingly losing control and hurtling toward me. With limited space to halt, I braked abruptly, steering the bike to the side. The other vehicle managed to stop just before colliding with mine. Although there was no damage, the incident served as a stark reminder to remain vigilant on the unpredictable mountain roads. I picked up my bike and started towards the top.

The ascent to ChangLa Pass unfolded as the most exhilarating and perilous leg of the journey. The rain intensified, accompanied by light snowfall, creating a mesmerizing yet challenging environment. The road, now riddled with water-filled potholes, bordered by snow-clad mountains on one side and a steep abyss on the other, added an element of fear to the thrill. Fellow bikers shared the excitement as we ascended together.

After an hour of cautious driving, around 1:30 PM, I reached the summit. Surprisingly, the top was bustling with numerous vehicles and a more substantial crowd than anticipated. Our traveler was parked ahead, and I carefully maneuvered my bike through the snowy terrain alongside the road. The entire summit was blanketed in snow, with fog obscuring the view of the descent. People were taking pictures and awaiting a clear weather window. We gathered at the center of ChangLa Pass, and suddenly, a heavy snowfall commenced. The snowfall was more intense than the rain encountered on the way to Pangong Lake.

Undeterred by the freezing temperatures, we danced and revealed in the snowfall, an experience none of us had encountered before. As the cold seeped in, we retreated into the warmth of the traveler to deliberate on our next move. Checking the temperature, I found it had already below zero. Safety became a paramount concern at this highest point of the mountain.

After waiting for a while inside the traveler, Tashi suggested descending as the snowfall showed no signs of abating. We collectively decided to embark on a slow and steady descent down the mountain together.

Amidst the relentless snowfall, my bike remained partially buried in a pristine layer of snow. As I brushed off the accumulated snow from the seat, I settled onto the bike, inadvertently allowing the remaining snow to melt and seep into my jacket. The cold moisture found its way into my shoes, and my hands, now half-numb, clutched the handlebars as I initiated the bike's engine.

Navigating the challenging landscape, the road presented a complex mosaic of potholes filled with snow, large stones lining one side, and an intensifying snowfall. Within minutes, the precipitation escalated to a deluge, heightening the difficulty of the journey. Fog began to accumulate inside my helmet, and the relentless snow made its way through. Frustratingly, I couldn't open the helmet's front to clear my vision. My hands, thoroughly numb, struggled with the handlebars, and my pants and shoes were thoroughly soaked.

The visibility ahead dwindled to the blinking lights of vehicles, making it an onerous task to navigate. In this challenging predicament, I persevered, opting for cautious driving in the first gear, relying on guesswork, the intermittent blinking lights, and the limited gap between the helmet and the front glass. The circumstances grew more daunting – fog within the helmet persisted, snow infiltrated, and the already compromised visibility made the journey even more perilous. Continuous cleaning of the helmet with one hand became a necessity. During turns, I resorted to lifting the helmet's glass to ensure there were no substantial obstacles like large stones on the road's side or oncoming traffic from the uphill direction.

Contemplating the idea of a temporary pause by the roadside to reassess the situation, I continued in this precarious state for the next 15-20 minutes until encountering an unexpected traffic jam up ahead.

Feeling a sense of relief, I eased my grip on the handlebars and brought the bike to a halt behind a line of vehicles. The cessation allowed me a moment to peel off my helmet, clearing it from accumulated snow, and I vigorously shook my hands to revive some semblance of feeling. The extremities had grown numb, making it challenging to operate the clutch and front brake – critical components in the perilous descent that lay ahead. As the traffic jam extended, I took advantage of the brief respite, taking in the surreal beauty of the heavy snowfall and the enveloping snow-capped mountains.

Despite the mesmerizing ambiance, the reality of navigating these treacherous conditions cast a shadow over the breathtaking scene. Snow continued to fall relentlessly, adding an element of both thrill and fear to the already adventurous journey. In this hostile environment, hunger became an afterthought, overshadowed by the urgency and caution required for the descent.

After approximately thirty minutes, the traffic jam dispersed, and I cautiously resumed my descent in first gear. The clock now approached 2 pm, and a sense of hunger gnawed at my consciousness. However, the pressing concern was the hazardous ride in the ongoing snowfall. The amalgamation of thrill, amazement, fear, and adventure created a potent cocktail of emotions. I silently hoped for the safe descent of my fellow bikers, each grappling with their own set of challenges.

While the climate painted a mesmerizing picture of heavy snowfall against a backdrop of snow-capped peaks, the practicality of navigating in such conditions was an arduous ordeal. The descent continued, the road becoming increasingly slippery, and the presence of snow-filled pits promised a bumpy ride until the base of the mountain.

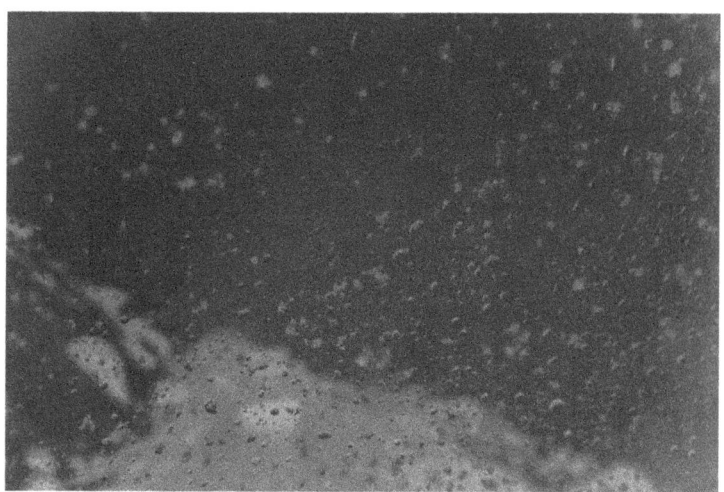

Helmet visibility at Chang La

Visibility dwindled further, and the snowfall intensified as I descended. The lack of a clear view posed additional challenges, yet there was a silver lining — fewer vehicles were ascending from the opposite direction. The road, now slick and skid-prone, posed a new set of challenges. My vision became increasingly obscured, relying solely on intermittent flashes of vehicle lights and a vague understanding of the road's trajectory. At this point, the snowfall, almost blizzard-like, transformed the descent into an exhilarating yet perilous adventure.

A few kilometers into the descent, I encountered a small group of people and a truck diligently working to clear the path. I sought information on the remaining distance, and with a reassurance that it was merely three kilometers to the base, a wave of relief washed over me. Ankit, arriving shortly after, shared the challenges he faced — his jacket was wet, and his hands had grown numb. The workers advised us to keep moving, highlighting the potential risks of stopping on the narrow, snow-laden road.

Despite the temptation to halt for a more extended period, considering the deteriorating weather conditions and the possibility of more vehicles approaching from behind, I decided to press on. Stopping amidst the snowfall might exacerbate the situation, potentially leading to an extended wait, if not a complete standstill.

With a renewed sense of determination, I recommenced the descent into the unknown, navigating with impaired visibility and relying on the sporadic illumination of headlights. My bike moved at a snail's pace, negotiating the road with caution, frequently entering snow-filled pits. The persistent numbness in my hands and legs served as a constant reminder of the harsh weather conditions.

As the journey unfolded, the snowfall showed no signs of abating. Blinking lights served as my only guide, and the route became increasingly challenging to discern. I forged ahead, the descent becoming a delicate dance between intuition and guesswork, my hands and legs operating on autopilot to manage the clutch and brake. The ordeal of feeling an almost complete loss of sensation in my extremities persisted, yet I soldiered on, inching closer to the base of the mountain.

In that moment, a realization dawned upon me – this experience, with all its challenges and uncertainties, was a unique chapter that might not repeat itself. Discarding thoughts of the worst-case scenario, I decided to embrace the situation and relish it as the most adventurous moment of the journey. Adopting this mindset brought a measure of calmness, allowing me to steer the bike with newfound assurance.

For the next half an hour, I maneuvered the bike through the challenging conditions, inching forward while the 3-kilometer milestone seemed perpetually out of reach. The earlier assurance about the remaining distance proved inaccurate, and the prolonged nature of the descent began to wear on my patience. Yet, the determination to find joy in the adventure persisted.

After another 20-30 minutes, the snow transitioned into a downpour, transforming the landscape and easing the strain on visibility. A sense of relief washed over me as the rain replaced the relentless snowfall. Navigating through the mountainous terrain, I decided to take a momentary break, pulling over to the side of the road. The sight of numerous vehicles descending reassured me, and consulting my mobile map revealed that I had covered nearly 50-60 kilometers of the challenging mountain road today.

As the rain continued to fall, the road ahead appeared to improve, signaling the likelihood of reaching the base without further snowfall. The tension began to dissipate, and a renewed sense of relaxation settled in. Contemplating an early start and a brief pause upon reaching the bottom, I resumed the journey. Over the next 2-3 kilometers, the road gradually transformed, offering smoother terrain and a distinct sense that the challenging descent was nearing its end.

Spotting our traveler and the bikes of fellow riders parked ahead, I followed suit, finding a suitable spot on the side of the road. A quick inspection revealed a layer of frozen ice on my legs below the knee, a testament to the intense cold and wet conditions. Removing the frozen layers, opening my gloves, and taking off the helmet, I sought refuge inside the warmth of the traveler.

Within, I found my fellow bikers already assembled. A collective shout of recognition filled the vehicle as we locked eyes and exchanged understanding glances. In that shared moment, only we, the bikers who had traversed the challenging descent, could truly comprehend the depth of our shared experience. The relief etched on each face mirrored my own, fostering a sense of camaraderie that transcended words. We lingered inside, basking in the warmth and relaxation, ultimately deciding to halt our journey in Sakti district, a mere 15 kilometers from our current location.

Descending from ChangLa pass, the change in environment was striking, and the thrill of conquering the challenging terrain lingered. Suddenly, a group of bikers approaching from the opposite direction flagged me down. Curious about the conditions ahead, they inquired whether it was safe to ascend to ChangLa pass. Advising caution, I suggested waiting for improved weather, emphasizing that the current conditions weren't conducive for a pleasant experience. Fortunately, they heeded the advice, opting to delay their ascent. Witnessing their decision brought a sense of contentment.

Resuming my journey, the sun began to emerge, gradually dispelling the lingering chill. Within the next 10-15 minutes, our group reached Sakti and parked near a welcoming restaurant. Eager to dry our jackets and shoes, we seized the opportunity to bask in the sunlight. Settling into a chair, the anticipation of a well-deserved meal heightened the sense of relaxation. We placed an order for momos and coffee, savoring the tantalizing aroma that filled the air. The 15-minute wait for our order became a cherished interlude, and when the coffee arrived, its rich flavor surpassed expectations. Opting for a second cup, I reveled in the satisfaction that only a good cup of coffee can bring – a sentiment echoed by Ankit.

As the steaming momos made their appearance, the tantalizing scent hinted at a culinary delight. Each bite seemed to embody vitality, perhaps enhanced by the juxtaposition of the recent adventure. Lingering at the restaurant for the next half-hour, we relished a momentary respite. The thought of a hot water shower beckoned, but Tashi urged us to continue our journey, emphasizing the need to reach the next destinations on the way to our overnight stay in Leh.

Gathering our belongings, we donned our jackets and shoes, readying ourselves for the road ahead. I kick-started my bike, taking the turn towards Leh just behind our traveler. Tashi, seemingly in a playful spirit, initiated a race with the traveler on the straight highway. Eager to embrace the smooth road, I accelerated, surpassing speeds of 110+ km/h in the next few minutes. The sensation was akin to savoring a delectable dessert after a challenging meal – the road was a delightful treat for a dedicated biker, unfolding smoothly for the next half-hour.

A view inside Leh city: Back to Hyderabad

सत्यं जीवनस्य सारथी यत्र अनुभवाः नयन्ति

Truth is the charioteer of life, where experiences lead

At approximately 5 pm, I brought my bike to a halt near the Thiksey Monastery, a prominent structure located near Leh. The monastery sprawled across the elevated landscape, its expansive area visible even from a distance. Despite its grandeur, I opted not to venture inside, considering that we had already explored one of the largest and most beautiful monasteries in Lumayuru/Diskit during our journey.

Shortly thereafter, our traveler pulled up beside me, and within the next five minutes, Pratiek and Rohit joined us. While awaiting Ankit's arrival, Tashi maneuvered the traveler towards the Thiksey Monastery. Parking on the side, I noticed Ankit had crossed the path unnoticed, possibly due to the speed at which he was riding. With no mobile device on him, as we shared the same SIM card network in my phone, a realization struck me after ten minutes – Ankit might have surged ahead. Deciding to continue our journey towards Leh, Pratiek and I informed the others to explore the monastery, considering our previous encounters with various monastic structures on the trip.

Starting our bikes, Pratiek and I embarked on the road to Leh, hoping to rendezvous with Ankit along the way. Approximately 10 km later, we spotted Ankit waiting on the side of the road. Eagerly parking our bikes, we basked in the sun for a while, the relief palpable upon confirming Ankit's well-being. Our next plan was to visit the school featured in the movie "3 Idiots," conveniently located about 5 km away.

On this occasion, as I kick-started my bike, the clutch emitted a distinctive sound at lower speeds. Reflecting on the day's ride across ChangLa Pass, I deduced that this might be the source of the issue. Despite the radiant sunshine and the ensuing sense of relaxation, I felt compelled to head back to the hotel.

Nevertheless, I was determined to explore the day's destinations, with the 3 Idiots school being a notable spot on the list. Within the next 10-15 minutes, our trio arrived at the school. I reached out to Tashi, discovering that they too were en route to the same destination. While waiting, the three of us decided to venture inside the school and take a spontaneous tour.

As we strolled through the premises, I couldn't help but notice familiar locations from scenes in the movie. The experience triggered a wave of nostalgia, prompting me to reminisce about my school and college days, briefly missing my old classmates. Engaging in a lighthearted exploration, we captured numerous photos, playfully posing amidst the scenic backdrops.

Before long, the rest of our friends joined us. We gathered for a group photo, and then continued to wander around, enjoying each other's company in this comprehensive setting of 3 Idiot's school.

Eager to retire to our hotel after an exhilarating and unexpected day of adventure, our group of bikers collectively sensed the fatigue that accompanied such an extraordinary drive. Although there were two more destinations on our list for the day – Shanti Stupa and Leh Palace – the allure of rest beckoned.

Shanti Stupa, a symbol of peace and tranquility, was constructed by Japanese Buddhists. The stupa is a magnificent sight, with a stunning Buddha statue at its base. The statue exudes a sense of serenity and calm, embodying the teachings of peace and harmony. Surrounded by the majestic Himalayan mountains and overlooking the beautiful city of Leh, the view from Shanti Stupa is simply breathtaking. The vast expanse of the sky above adds to the grandeur of the scene, creating a sense of awe and reverence. It's a place that inspires reflection and contemplation, inviting visitors to find inner peace amidst the beauty of nature.

Opting for a moment of reprieve, I observed as the others embarked on a visit to Shanti Stupa. From my vantage point outside, it appeared akin to other stupas I had encountered in India, reminiscent of one I explored in Odisha just two months prior. The distinguishing factor lay in the breathtaking surroundings of mountains that enveloped this particular monastery. As our friends explored the peaceful structure, I, accompanied by Ankit, started making my way towards the Leh palace.

Meenal, who had visited Leh Palace before reuniting with us at Sangam River, shared her experiences and knowledge about the palace in a captivating manner. Her explanations painted a vivid picture of the palace's history and significance. As we approached our lodging, Leh Palace loomed large in the distance, its ancient walls bearing witness to over 400 years of history since its construction around 1600. The palace stood as a silent sentinel, offering a panoramic view of the entire city of Leh from its vantage point. Leh palace gives a sense of tranquility, as if the palace itself exuded a peaceful aura. The interiors were adorned with paintings and statues that showcased the rich Tibetan culture of bygone eras. Each brushstroke and carving seemed to tell a story of a bygone era, offering a glimpse into the past.

However, the aftermath of our snowy escapade clung to us, seeping through jackets and shoes, leaving us thoroughly chilled. A sense of dampness and coldness prevailed within, a stark reminder of the wintry adventure that had left its mark on our bodies.

At approximately 6:30 pm, I wearily arrived at the hotel, a culmination of a day filled with thrilling adventures and unexpected twists. The first order of business was to shed the protective gear, meticulously removing the knee and elbow guards. I entrusted the hotel manager with their safekeeping, ensuring they would find their way back to the bike vendors.

With an eagerness to cast off the remnants of the day's exploits, I hastened into the hotel room. In a swift sequence, my shoes were discarded, replaced by the comfort of half pants. Anticipating the rejuvenating effects of warmth, I procured a bucket of piping hot water and strategically placed it near the window. Seating myself on a chair, I immersed my fatigued legs into the invigorating heat, relishing the immediate sense of relief that permeated my entire body.

In tandem, Ankit indulged in a therapeutic shower, also opting for the comforting embrace of hot water. As I basked in the warmth by the window, I seized the opportunity to make a call home, reassuring my loved ones of our safe return and regaling them with tales of the awe-inspiring journey. Word reached me that Pratiek and Rohit had rejoined us at the hotel, their weariness mirroring ours, prompting a collective desire for a revitalizing shower.

Meanwhile, our other travel companions, predominantly the female contingent, embarked on a shopping expedition to the bustling markets of Leh. Politely declining their invitation to join, I expressed my intention to partake in the post-shower camaraderie. The act of immersing oneself in the comforting cascade of hot water turned out to be an unparalleled luxury, akin to a soothing balm for the body and soul. It felt as though each droplet of warmth expelled the lingering chill from every corner of my being, making it the most indulgent and prolonged shower of my life.

Post-shower, I reclined on the bed for half an hour, allowing the fatigue of the day to gradually dissipate. While the prospect of exploring the vibrant Leh market beckoned, my current inclination was to introspect and savor the lingering moments of solitude, contemplating the profound experiences of the trip thus far.

At around 8 pm, Ankit and I descended to the dining area for dinner, greeted by the chef who informed us that the food was ready and awaiting our arrival. Seizing the opportunity, we decided to explore Leh market, which was conveniently situated near our accommodation. The market, vast and extensive, offered a plethora of local treasures. Intrigued, I indulged in purchasing flags and other specialties unique to Leh, while also treating myself to some delectable local non-vegetarian dishes.

Our stroll through the market extended for an hour, filled with the discovery of local gems and the savoring of regional flavors. Returning to the hotel just in time for dinner, my appetite remained robust despite having sampled snacks in the market. Within the next 10-15 minutes, the rest of our companions trickled in from their market expedition, culminating in a final gathering for dinner.

Gathered around the table for the last communal meal of the trip, a member of the hotel staff graciously served our food. Conversations flowed, centered around the experiences of the Leh market and the various items acquired during our shopping escapade. The shared enjoyment of the meal, complemented by a special dessert, marked a fitting conclusion to our culinary experiences on the journey.

Given the weariness accumulated from the day's travels, the collective decision was made to retire to our respective rooms for a well-deserved night's rest. Anticipating an early departure for Leh Airport the following morning, we bid each other goodnight, cherishing the memories of a trip that had brought us together and provided a tapestry of unforgettable experiences.

Rising with the first light around 6 am, I found myself emerging from a deep and restful slumber. The morning held a tranquility that resonated with the warmth of Leh, a stark contrast to the more rugged stay at Pangong Lake. As I descended to partake in a soothing cup of tea bathed in the soft sunlight, a sense of relaxation enveloped me. Yet, amid the comfort of the Leh stay, my thoughts lingered on the adventures of the previous day, contemplating the imminent conclusion of the journey.

Returning to my room, I indulged in a refreshing shower and set about packing my belongings. At breakfast, a collective assembly of fellow travelers with laden luggage marked the realization that our time in Leh was drawing to a close. Tashi, our trusted driver and companion throughout the trip, had already begun the task of loading our bags into the traveler.

Amid the bittersweet atmosphere of our final breakfast in Leh, nostalgia and the awareness of the journey's end hung in the air. Some of us decided to seize the remaining moments for a swift shopping excursion in the market. Post-breakfast, we promptly embarked on our shopping mission, urging Tashi to pick us up on our way to the airport.

This impromptu shopping spree was a swift and crucial endeavor, a last-minute opportunity to acquire souvenirs and essentials that a few had missed the evening before. With our purchases in tow, Tashi collected us, and we made our way towards the airport. Anticipating our departure, I couldn't help but recall hearing about the airport's reputation—it was touted as one of the most beautiful airports in India. The final leg of our journey was underway, blending a sense of farewell with the anticipation of witnessing the renowned beauty of Leh Airport.

As we traversed the corridors of Leh Airport, surrounded by the awe-inspiring panorama of snow-capped peaks, the grandeur of the natural landscape seemed to whisper tales of our recent conquests on two wheels. The very mountains that had challenged us just days ago now stood as silent sentinels bidding us farewell. Each step within the airport terminal echoed with the memories of laughter, camaraderie, and the indomitable spirit that defined our time in Leh.

Upon entering the terminal, the familiar rituals of security checks unfolded. In this routine, Meenal, one of our fellow travelers, encountered a brief delay as her luggage underwent additional scrutiny. Amidst the bustling activity, a peculiar scene unfolded involving a couple whose baggage contained a surprising surplus of daily essentials—multiple tubes of toothpaste, an eclectic array of shampoos, washing powders, and even oxygen gas boxes. The husband, maintaining a composed demeanor, silently obliged the security protocols, while his vocal wife expressed her dissatisfaction with the situation.

Undeterred by the momentary diversion, we proceeded toward Gate No.2 for boarding, knowing that it was time to bid adieu to Leh's captivating landscapes. The experiences of our journey, etched in our collective consciousness, added a layer of sentimentality to our departure. The joy and warmth of the moments shared during our stay promised to endure in the recesses of our memories for a lifetime.

Navigating the boarding process, we found our seats aboard the aircraft bound for Delhi. Special care was afforded to Meenal, ensuring her journey continued smoothly. Securing a window seat, I aimed to capture the final glimpses of the mesmerizing landscapes from above, cherishing the intricate tapestry of nature that had become an integral part of our shared adventure.

As the aircraft taxied down the runway, I gazed out the window, contemplating the profound impact of the journey and expressing gratitude for the beauty and camaraderie that had accompanied us from Leh's soaring peaks to the skies above.

The spectacle that unfolded beneath the wings of the aircraft was nothing short of breathtaking. A vast expanse of snow-capped mountains stretched as far as the eye could see, a mesmerizing panorama that seemed to defy the ordinary. These were mountains devoid of the lush foliage of trees, their naked peaks reaching towards the heavens. As I peered out of the window, a surge of emotions welled up within me, a mix of awe and amusement, realizing that not long ago, I had navigated the winding roads of these very mountains astride my trusty bike. The landscapes that once challenged and inspired me now lay sprawled beneath, a testament to the journey that had unfolded just day ago.

The aerial perspective added a new layer of appreciation to the rugged beauty of Leh's topography. Each peak, ridge, and valley told a story of resilience and grandeur, and I couldn't help but marvel at the vastness of the landscape that had been my playground on two wheels. The scenes unfolding below were beyond the realms of conventional thinking, an out-of-the-box experience that left an indelible mark on my senses.

For the next half an hour, we were treated to an uninterrupted visual symphony as the aircraft glided gracefully above Leh. The play of light and shadow on the undulating mountains painted a picture of unparalleled beauty. It was a shared moment of appreciation among fellow travelers, each of us silently contemplating the majesty of the Himalayas from this unique vantage point. The memories of our journey, etched into the landscapes we now soared above, added a layer of profundity to the experience, making this final leg of the trip a poetic reflection on the remarkable adventure that had unfolded beneath these very skies.

In the ensuing half-hour, our descent brought us to the bustling city of Delhi. A subtle awareness permeated the cabin, reminding us that the temperature shift awaiting us would be quite drastic from the cool climes of Leh. As the aircraft touched down on the Delhi runway, the pilot's announcement rang through the cabin, declaring a stark contrast in temperature—36 degrees Celsius, a considerable leap from the 1-2 degrees we had grown accustomed to in Leh. Stepping off the aircraft, the surge of hot air enveloped us like a sudden blast of heat, a sharp transition from the crisp mountain air.

Hastily boarding the bus, the air-conditioned refuge provided a welcome respite from the Delhi heat. The rush to escape the sun's intensity mirrored the collective sentiment of the passengers. Inside the bus, there was a palpable sense of relief as we anticipated the next leg of our journey—retrieving our checked-in luggage from belt no. 3.

With our flight to Hyderabad scheduled for the evening, the atmosphere was more relaxed for me and Ankit. The same applied to the group of Pune girls who also had evening flights. Gathering near the baggage claim, we seized the opportunity for a final round of group photos, capturing the essence of our shared adventure.

However, it was time for some goodbyes. The Mumbai friends, bound for their train journey, had to depart early, leaving the six of us with a free afternoon ahead. With our flight departure hours away, we decided to make the most of the time and enjoy a leisurely lunch together at a nearby spot. Boarding a bus toward the Aerocity center near Terminal 1 Airport, we found ourselves at a bustling food plaza. There, surrounded by the diverse aromas and flavors, we indulged in a variety of dishes, savoring not just the food but also the camaraderie that had defined our journey. The laughter and conversations echoed the memories we had forged together, marking a fitting conclusion to our extraordinary adventure before embarking on the final leg of our journey back home.

Our fellow travelers, Dhanashri and Swaralee, had been craving non-vegetarian fare, a longing that had grown during the trip where most of our meals had been predominantly vegetarian. The food plaza at Aerocity presented the perfect opportunity to satiate their appetite for non-veg delights. Amidst a delightful spread of flavors, we immersed ourselves in the culinary experience, relishing the diverse menu for the next one to two hours.

With our flight looming on the horizon, scheduled for around 7 pm, we decided to leave Aerocity by 4 o'clock. Tapasya's brother, a resident of Delhi, had come to pick her up, as she planned to extend her stay in the capital for a few more days before heading back to Pune. Meanwhile, Ankit and I, along with the others, opted to book a cab for Terminal 3 at the Delhi airport.

As we made our way to Terminal 3, we dropped off Dhanasri, Swarali, and Chaitanya, who were departing from Terminal 3. It was a moment of farewells and well-wishes as they headed towards their departure gate. Terminal 3 served as the nexus for their onward journey.

Subsequently, Ankit and I found ourselves walking from Terminal 3 to Terminal 1. Conveniently, both terminals are within reasonable walking distance from each other. The transition between terminals became a reflective stroll, allowing us to savor the remnants of our shared adventure, the laughter, the camaraderie, and the multitude of experiences that had defined this remarkable journey. As we approached Terminal 1, the anticipation of our evening flight mingled with the sentiment of bidding adieu to the fellow travelers who had become companions on this unforgettable odyssey.

Navigating through the airport, my focus shifted momentarily as Dhansari's call disrupted the routine of my departure. Her voice carried a hint of tension as she unraveled the story of their flight cancellation, a predicament that unfolded days before in Leh when network issues prevented them from accessing the critical email notification.

Empathy surged within me as I listened to the challenges they faced in trying to rectify the situation with the airline. It was a testament to the unpredictable nature of travel, especially in remote regions like Leh, where communication hurdles could unexpectedly impact even the best-laid plans.

Inside the airport, I took it upon myself to inquire about potential alternative flights to Pune. The bustling terminal became a hub of information as I sought out options and explored potential solutions. An hour into the inquiry, Dhanshri reached out once again, her tone now carrying a palpable sense of relief. They had successfully secured a flight for the night, albeit at a higher cost.

The news brought a collective sigh of relief. The unforeseen hiccup had been navigated, and a resolution was found. As I continued through the airport procedures, the incident underscored the unpredictable nature of travel and the importance of adaptability. It became a subtle reminder that, in the realm of exploration, challenges may arise, but solutions often emerge, reshaping the journey and adding unexpected layers to the tapestry of experiences.

In the subsequent half-hour, Ankit and I found ourselves settled comfortably in our flight, embarking on the journey back to Hyderabad. The fatigue from the eventful trip caught up with me, prompting a welcome respite as I succumbed to the lull of slumber for the next two hours. As the flight descended to the familiar landscapes of

Hyderabad, I gradually awoke, feeling a renewed sense of homecoming.

Upon touchdown, we promptly booked a cab to transport us to our flat. The journey from the airport to my residence spanned an hour, during which I found myself in quiet reflection, mentally retracing the myriad landscapes and experiences of Leh-Ladakh. The familiar sight of my flat welcomed me, and upon entering, a wave of warmth enveloped me, contrasting the cool mountain air that still lingered in my memory.

Settling into a chair, I took a moment to savor the tranquility of my room. In that serene ambiance, I decided to brew a cup of green tea, the soothing aroma filling the air. As I sat there, contemplating the journey that had just concluded, an idea sparked in my mind—capturing these vivid memories through writing. Though it took a few weeks for the thought to fully crystallize, here it is—an attempt to immortalize the essence of the Leh-Ladakh trip.

Writing these reflections serves as a testament to the satisfaction derived from the journey, a mosaic of landscapes, challenges, and camaraderie. The act of chronicling this adventure breathes life into the memories, preserving them in a tangible form. To those reading, thank you for joining me on this narrative. I sincerely hope that the spirit of exploration and the allure of Leh-Ladakh beckon you to embark on your own adventure soon.

Journeys Shared: Reflection of Fellow Travelers

हृदयेन संयुक्तं, मैत्रीयां अनन्तम्

United in heart, infinite in friendship

Visiting Leh Ladakh with my sister and a group of new friends was an unforgettable experience that left a lasting impact on me. The breathtaking beauty of the snowcapped mountains served as a constant reminder of the vastness and serenity of the natural world. In the company of my companions, we shared laughter, explored charming destinations, had meals together, and formed deep bonds that will remain with me for a lifetime. This adventure allowed me to not only appreciate the wonders of nature but also the power of friendship and connection. Amidst the rugged landscapes and picturesque valleys, I discovered a sense of peace and tranquility that I had been seeking for a long time. The stunning surroundings provided the perfect backdrop for moments of deep introspection and self-reflection. It was during this journey that I truly understood the value of silence and how it can nourish the soul. Whether it was marveling at the architectural wonders of ancient monasteries or immersing myself in the vibrant local culture, each moment was an opportunity to embrace the richness of the present and find solace in the stillness. As the days went by, I realized that this trip to Leh Ladakh was not just about exploring a new destination, but also about exploring myself. In the midst of unfamiliar surroundings and with the support and encouragement of my fellow travelers, I stepped out of my comfort zone and embraced new experiences. This adventure taught me the importance of embracing spontaneity, finding joy in the little things, and celebrating every moment. Overall, my journey to Leh Ladakh was a transformative experience that not only broadened my horizons but also ignited a newfound sense of wonder and gratitude within me.

– Swaralee, @swarascape_

For me this trip has been nothing but a pool of adventures, one that I cannot forget in my lifetime, and will have multiple stories to tell to my forthcoming generations, love, fun ,drama, humor, togetherness, emotions everything combined, and turned out to be a super trip! a group trip which turns out to be a solo trip when I missed my flight to Srinagar but life also gave me a chance to explore things on my own, explore local culture, the warmth of the people, I had become an explorer for those 2 days eating in an army mess, being welcomed by army guys and being the only girl, getting my pictures clicked by cute Kashmiri folks, and roaming the streets making everyone my friend, there is a lot of warmth and welcoming nature in the Ladakhi's people, same concept as of Kashmir, anyone who goes there apart from exploring the terrain should actually explore the culture and would find some of the most beautiful memories that they would cherish for life, as i did.

— Meenal, @meenalkumari

या पृथ्वीवर काही स्थळे ही कायमच वलयांकित राहतील आणि त्यांना पाहण्याचे स्वर्ग सुख मनात असूनही विविध कारणांनी पूर्ण होण्याचा योग मात्र येत नाही.

असेच एकदा माझी मैत्रीण चैतन्याचा मेसेज आला आणि तो पाहून आश्चर्याने डोळे चमकले नसते तर शप्पत. तो भन्नाट मेसेज होता एक ट्रिप चा आणि अनेक विचार विनिमयाअंती प्लॅन ठरलाच- लेह लडाख च्या सहलीचा 🐱

पुण्यापासून सुरु झालेला हा प्रवास पावलोपावली कायम च आव्हानात्मक ठरला. दिल्लीहून भल्या पहाटे मस्त आवरून निघालेलो आम्ही मीनल च्या चुकामुकीमुळे भलतेच नाराज झालो. पुढे कारगिल ला जाताना तर आपले आयुष्यात एकदा तरी बर्फ पाहायला मिळावा हे स्वप्न पूर्ण होताना पाहून अगदी वेड च लागले. त्यानंतर पुढील काही दिवस अगदी फ्रीज मधील बर्फ पण

पाहण्याची इच्छा नाही उरली हे मात्र वेगळे सांगायला नको😊. या अशा बर्फाळ प्रदेशात प्रतिकूल परिस्थितीत आपले सैनिक कसे सीमेवर लढत असतील या विचाराने डोळे नकळत पाणावले.

पुढे खारदुंग ला, चांग ला अशा ठिकाणी तर सर्वांचाच कस लागला. समोर नयनमनोहर दृश्य तर होतीच पण गोल घाटवळणीचे रस्ते, असह्य थंडी, ऑक्सिजन ची कमतरता, खाण्याची आबाळ(₹२०० ची मॅगी🍜 पण तरी आम्ही खाल्लीच😋) हे सारे पाहता "ये कहां आ गये हम..." बस हेच गाणे सारखे आठवायचे. पण हसी-मजाक आणि फोटोशूट करत प्रवास सुकर होत गेला. एव्हाना सर्वांचे बाँडिंग ही छान जमलेले हे वेगळे सांगायला नको.

शांतिस्तुप,भव्य दिव्य बुद्धमूर्ती, कारगिल मेमोरिअल, दल लेक, पत्थर साहेब गुरुद्वारा, बर्फवृष्टी आणि बर्फाचे डोंगर, निळाशार आणि गोठवणारा pangong लेक व तेथील गुलाबी साडीतील तपस्याचे फोटोशूट, चैतन्याची अचानक बिघडलेली तब्बेत आणि तिला मदत म्हणून नवीन ने ऑफर केलेली बुलेट राईड, मार्केट मधील घसघीस करत केलेले शॉपिंग, आयुष्यात पहिल्यांदा खाल्लेले 'व्हेज मोमोज', स्नेहल चा मोबाईल हरवल्यावर झालेला हिरमोड, नीट जॅकेट-शूज नसतानाही आमच्या बाईकर बॉइज ने केलेला प्रवास आणि लास्ट बट नॉट द लिस्ट, नुब्रा व्हॅली सारख्या ठिकाणी केक अरेंज करून माझी लेक ओशिन चा व्हर्चुअली सेलिब्रेट केलेला वाढदिवस या सर्व आठवणी कायमसाठी माझ्या मनात कोरल्या गेल्या आहेत.

या ट्रिप ने फक्त कडू गोड अनुभव च दिले असे नाही तर नवीन-अंकित-प्रतीक-रोहित-तपस्या-साक्षी-मीनल सारखे मित्रमैत्रीण आणि लहान बहीणीसम स्नेहल हे सारे काही भेटवले. बहीण स्वराली आणि चैतन्या या दोघी तर सोबत आहेत ना मग बाकी टेन्शन नाही, असे म्हणत केलेला हा प्लॅन आयुष्यभरासाठी एक अद्भुत अनुभव ठरला.

खरी मजा(का सजा 😅?) तर तेव्हा आली जेव्हा दिल्ली हून पुण्यासाठीची फ्लाईटच एक महिन्यापूर्वी रद्द झालीये हे कळाले. खरं तर हे ऐकून तर पायाखालची जमीनच सरकलेली पण तरी तेव्हा कसे बसे तिकीट बुकिंग वाल्यांचे पाय पडत ३ तिकीटे मिळवली. विमान पुण्यात पोहोचले तेव्हा कुठे हुश्श झाले. 😌

लहानपणापासून आत्तापर्यंत भारतातील बऱ्याच प्रेक्षणीय स्थळांना भेटी झाल्या पण माझा अनुभव अशाप्रकारे शब्दात मांडण्याचा एक नवीन प्रयत्न आज पहिल्यांदाच "नवीन" मुळे साकार झाला.☺

निसर्गाचे विविधांगी दर्शन, लडाखी जीवन व जवानांच्या दर्शनाने पुनित करणाऱ्या लेह लडाखची भटकंती आयुष्यात एकदा तरी अनुभवावी अशीच आहे.

I Dreamt, I Explored and I found a treasure...Leh Ladakh!

There are some things that cannot be put into words. Love is one of them and then there is Ladakh- the land of scenic beauty, rustic charm, and nature at its best. It was the ultimate experience without breaking the bank!

My friends Naveen, Chitanya, Tapasya, Snehal, Pratiek and Swara played a vital role in making this trip memorable. I simply can't forget my daughter's birthday surprise cake they arranged during the Nubra Valley stay. It was emotional yet the best moment of the trip.

Though traveling to Leh-Ladakh is a breathtaking and awe-inspiring journey through dramatic landscapes and rich cultural heritage, one must experience this at least once in life.

- Dhanashree Mahirrao, @dhanaashree_nikhil

Ladakh trip is the dream of their lifetime for every passionate bike rider. This trip was a mix-up of adventure, thrill and lot of unexpected events. Best part of this group is the essence of family bond where everyone is ready to support each other in their worst whether it is oxygen deficiency, extreme cold weather, or supporting each other in their special moments. This trip was my dream trip, but I made a family here which will be remembered for this lifetime and are an important part of me. This trip's special moment for me was the night we spent in pangong lake where there was extreme cold temperature, everyone was uneasy still we danced in that situation as a family. Thank you each and everyone for giving me these beautiful moments and making this trip more special!!!

- Rohit Kadam, @mrbeardenfielder_official

It indeed a paradise on the earth, though no picture can do justice to the magic that Ladakh spells on your mind and so it was always in my bucket list. I still remember it was month of May and my Trek friend, Rohit, asked me "Leh-Ladakh chale kya". I was like let's plan it and from there the hustle started- planning itinerary to find better travel groups, negotiations all the credit goes to Rohit. Last year in June, I went to get in the beauty of Ladakh. That was epic of the journey which is kind of hard to forget. There were a lot of epic moments which are hard to express, one can only feel them.

One of the most memorable moments was enjoying a full snowfall at Khardungla Pass (highest motarable Road in the world) at a height of 18380 ft. As I am into trekking, this was my highest feet yet till date. These snow-covered roads leading to these higher passes brings you closer to yourself and forget the reality of world.

Second most memorable moment was that of seeing formation of 7 colors on the crystal-clear water of PANGONG Lake. It was mesmerizing and we were fortunate enough as it was full moon night. Weather was clear with sun shining in the afternoon and night we experienced snowfall too. We were there to witness the rocky lofty mountains turning snowcapped. AMS (Acute Mountain sickness) also took control over me. So, take a good care of hydration. But all was well, we care all of us and everyone has completed it very well.

– Sakshi, @sakshiraj.raj3

माझा लेह लदाखचा अविस्मरणीय प्रवास....

ह्या ट्रिपचा अनुभव काही वेगळाच होता अतिशय अविस्मरणीय असे ते सोनेरी दिवस आणि त्यातील प्रत्येक क्षण✦✧☁...स्वप्नातील जग जे आजपर्यंत फोटोत किंवा टी व्ही वर बघत होतो ते दृश्य स्वतःच्या डोळ्यांनी प्रत्यक्ष अनुभवले त्या क्षणी मनात जे भाव वाटत होते त्या भावना शब्दात व्यक्त करण खरतर अवघड आहे शब्द अपुरे पडतील असे ते दिवस ... उंचच उंच पर्वतरांगा तिथले ते मोकळे रस्ते तिथल्या निसर्गाची शोभाच काही वेगळी न्यारी आहे. तिथल्या विविधतेने नटलेली धार्मिक स्थळ, निलेशार आभाळ , अथांग असे समुद्र आजही ती दृश्य डोळ्यासमोर आहेत. आणि त्यात सोन्याहून पिवळ म्हणजे त्या प्रवासात सोबती म्हणून लाभलेले सगळे मित्र मैत्रिणी...काही ओळखीचे तर काही अनोळखी पण 1 क्षणही अस कोणी जाणवू नाही दिल की कोणी अनोळखी आहोत. इतके प्रेमळ, जिवाला जीव लावणारे जिव्हाळ्याचे जिवलग मित्रमैत्रिणी नशिबानेच मिळतात असे म्हणायला काही हरकत नाही. इतकी मजा मस्ती दंगा हसून खेळून सगळे होते की ते 5-6 दिवस कसे निघून गेले काही कळ्ळलच नाही मात्र त्या दिवसात ह्या सगव्व्या मित्रमैत्रिणीनी आयुष्यभर लक्षात राहतील असे अविस्मरणीय क्षण आठवणी देऊन गेले. जे आजही आठवले की मन पुन्हा धावत तिथे जाऊन पोहोचते.0 degree जिथे पहिली Adventur Snow मधे ATV bike Ride Keli जणू काही बर्फाच्या दुनियेत गेल्यासारखे वाटत होते चारही बाजूने बर्फाच्या डोंगर रांगा... नंतर Go-kart ride, Pangong lake वेगवेगळ्या Props सोबत काढलेले फोटो, कारगीलची ती गरम गरम इन्स्टंट maggi, Bike Ride, बसच्या टपावर उभ राहून काढलेले फोटो, मार्केटमध्ये जाऊन धावतपळत केलेली शॉपिंग😊 असे सगळ करत करत प्रवास पुढे पुढे जात होता आणि अंतर मात्र कमी होत होत.

Bike वर त्या लेह लदाखच्या रस्त्यांवरून खासकरून khardungla आणि changla Pass फिरण्याची मज्जाच काही वेगळी होती सगळ्या मिश्र भावना खूपसारा आनंद ☺ बर्फातून धुक्यातून Bike Ride जातानाची थोडीशी भीती ☺ आणि तिथला निसर्ग तो अनुभवच मनाला आनंदाने तृप्त करणारा होता..Pangong lake ची गोठवून टाकणारी ती थंडी आजही आठवली तर अंगाला शहारे येतात❑❑ पण तरीही त्या थंडीला न जुमानता फोटो काढायसाठीची चाललेली धडपड काही वेगळीच होती☺🐝आणि तिथेच रात्री होटेलमधे सगळ्यांनी केलेला चद्दर Dance 💃 त्याला कसलीच तोड नाही❑❑. ह्या सगळ्यात आणखी 1 कायम लक्षात राहणारा माझा वाईट अनुभव म्हणजे Bike Ride वर असताना माझा फोन हरवला . सोबतच्या मित्र मैत्रिणीचे फोटो व्हिडिओ काढत असताना कधी माझा फोन हरवला काही समजलच नाही आणि फोनला Network नसल्यामुळे तो शोधण्यासाठीची तगमग काही विचारायला नको मग पुन्हा अर्धा रस्ता माघे गेलो फोन शोधत शोधत..तरी फोन काही मिळाला नाही त्याक्षणी माझे अश्रू अनावर झाले कारण त्यात संपूर्ण trip च्या आठवणी होत्या. फोन हरवल्यामुळे तिथल्या पोलिस स्टेशनला ही भेट देऊन झाली☺कायम लक्षात राहणारी अशीही 1 आठवण कायम आठवणीत राहील☺ आणि तिथूनच कानाला खडा लावला की इथून पुढे कुठेही जाताना फोन मात्र नीट सांभाळून ठेवायचा❑☺☺. Mumbai to delhi then Srinagar, Kargil, Leh ,Nubra valley, Pangong lake then again leh अस सगळ फिरून झाल्यावर मग परतीचा प्रवास सुरू झाला.पण जसा trip चा शेवट जवळ येत होता तेव्हा वाटत होत ही वेळ नको जायला.. वेळ थांबायला हवी..सगळ्यांना जणू पुन्हा घरचे परतीचे रस्ते दिसू लागले आणि मन थोडशांत झालं की थोड्यावेळात आपण सगळे आपापल्या शहरात, घरी, कामात व्यस्त होऊन जाऊ ह्या सगळ्या विचारांनीच मनात खळबळ केली होती कसबस मनाला सावरत पुन्हा शेवटच्या रात्री हॉटेल मधे UNO card game, धनश्रीच्या मुलीचा surprise bday, DAMSHARAS ती धमाल मस्ती त्याची मजाच काही वेगळी होती सगळ्यांचे गाल आणि पोट दुखेपर्यंतचे हसरे चेहरे आजही आठवले की आपोआप चेह-यावर हसू येतं आणि पुन्हा सगळ्यांनी लवकर भेटावे ही ओढ लागते. आजही मला प्रतीक्षा आहे त्या क्षणाची की कधी आम्ही सगळे एकत्र येऊ आणि असाच आणखी 1 अविस्मरणीय प्रवास सोबत घालवू...Miss You So Much Buddies."I am blessed to have such lovely people in my life. Thank you all for being a part of it. "Lots and lots of love to you all" ♡ 🫂

— Snehal Masavkar, @snehal_1125

"Ladakh is not a place..it's an emotion.

Where one can easily get lost in the captivating landscapes, where every view is a masterpiece, and every moment feels like a dream. Embarking on the long-awaited journey to visit Leh-Ladakh with an incredible group of people was a dream come true. "Changla Pass" where the mountains touch the sky and dreams touch reality. Every twist and turn on that mountainous road reinforced the notion that life is fragile and every decision counts.

You must have heard a lot about altitude Mountain sickness, where you feel symptoms at higher altitude levels. So let me tell you one thing... It's Real...!! It all started with headache and nausea, which might be more due to constant changing weather in Ladakh. The temperature is unpredictable. So, one should listen to your body and do not overexert yourself.

I would like to express my heartfelt gratitude to Meenal, who has been the epitome of care and support throughout this journey. Sakshi, our dedicated doctor, in providing medical assistance whenever needed. Tapasya, a strong-willed individual, has been an inspiration to us all. Snehal, our talkative companion, has kept us entertained with her lively conversations. Rohit, our reliable team leader, has guided us every step of the way. Prateik, the entertainer of our group, has never failed to bring smiles to our faces. Dhana, my buddy throughout this experience, has been a constant source of support. Swara, my little sister on this trip, has added joy and warmth to our adventures. Naveen, always helpful and kind-hearted, has made this journey easier for all of us. And lastly, Ankit, whose unwavering support has played a crucial role in helping me navigate through this challenging situation. Their collective support and assistance have been invaluable, enabling me to cope with and overcome the difficulties faced along the way.

IN SELFLESS ACTS, HEARTS ALIGHT,

KINDNESS BLOOMS, SHINING BRIGHT ☺

Despite the challenges, the thrill of conquering filled me with an unparalleled sense of accomplishment and gratitude. It was a moment of triumph that will forever be ingrained in my memory, serving as a reminder to seize every opportunity and embrace life's adventures with unwavering courage. Our journey took us further into the remote reaches of Ladakh, to the mesmerizing Pangong Lake. Nestled between towering mountains, the lake stretched out before us like a vast expanse of liquid sapphire. With each passing hour, the colors of the lake shifted and danced in the sunlight, revealing shades of turquoise, emerald, and cobalt blue. We spent the day exploring the lakeshore, skipping stones and soaking in the serenity of this otherworldly landscape.

Reflecting on this trip, I am reminded of the bonds forged, the laughter shared, and the indelible imprint it has left on my soul. It's moments like these that make life truly extraordinary, and I am grateful for the opportunity to have experienced it with such remarkable companions. This trip to Leh-Ladakh will always hold a special place in my heart, serving as a testament to the power of friendship, resilience, and the sheer beauty of the human spirit.

- Chaitanya, @chaitanyaemjal

For many years, I've dreamed of going to Ladakh with my friends after college. We tried many times, but it never happened. Finally, last year on June 3rd, we made it to Kashmir, and our trip began. It started on June 1st when we left Mumbai. Some friends I met for the first time. But by the end of the trip, we were like old friends.

One thing bothered me a bit, our friend Meenal, who missed her flight from Delhi to Jammu on the first day. We wondered how she'd manage alone for three days but she surprised us, and she was fine.

Everything else was amazing. As we explored Ladakh for 7-8 days, we had a lot of fun. Visiting Khardung La Pass was unforgettable, even though it was freezing cold and snowing heavily. But Chang La Pass was even scarier. It was freezing, and there was so much snow. Our hands and feet were numb. We managed to cross it, though, riding our powerful Himalayan bike. One night at Pangong Lake was super cold. We danced despite the cold.

We played games and celebrated birthdays. It felt like we formed a new family on this trip. Overall, it was a fantastic trip.

This was my dream trip, and I'm grateful to all my friends who made it special.

– Pratiek, @pratiek77

Finally, I did the most anticipated road trip to Ladakh which was years into making. Yes! I drove motorcycle myself for several days and I'm proud of it. One should be because it's kind of an amazing experience when you move towards those high-altitude landscapes. Specifically, if you appreciate a rider skill then it gets more special. Traveling to Leh was perhaps one of the most thrilling road adventures of my life upto to this point or for that matter will be the most exhilarating life experience in my whole life.

As, I reminisce the Jackets were on and sunglasses were out as me and my friend Naveen drove our bikes looking upward to the sky, strolled across several lakes, mountains, enjoyed the breeze, tried to catch as many colors as possible and experience lot of different weathers in that whole week. We took a back-breaking journey on broken mountain roads but none of us seemed to mind it.

The road trip might not have happened if Naveen had not pressed me to do it but I am glad I went as it was a life experience which I will be sharing even with my grandkids. Moreover, I was able to meet so many amazing new people with whom I shared this wonderful trip and made lifelong bonds with them. Besides I am hoping my coming adventures will be as exciting as this one or at least try to match it.

"Invest in Experience, not in things", this is what I believe in and this trip cemented my life mantra.

– Ankit Tyagi

Leh Ladakh holds a special place in my heart, as it has been a dream destination of mine for seven long years. Initially, I had envisioned exploring its breathtaking landscapes on a motorcycle with my partner. But I embarked on this adventure with my friends instead. Despite the change in plans, the experience was nothing short of extraordinary.

From navigating the exhilarating roads of Ladakh to facing unexpected challenges, such as Meenal missing her flight on the first day, Snehal losing her phone, and Chaitanya battling continuous bouts of vomiting, every moment was memorable. Amidst these trials, the highlight of the trip was fulfilling a long-standing dream of mine – wearing a saree at Pangong Lake and attempting to recreate a cherished memory.

Despite the freezing cold making it difficult to even move our fingers, I proudly draped the saree and struck poses, knowing it was far from the conventional way of doing so. This moment marked the culmination of years of anticipation and the fulfillment of a personal goal.

Leh Ladakh's beauty lies not only in its picturesque landscapes but also in the challenges it presents, making every journey an unforgettable adventure. Crossing it off my bucket list was a moment of immense satisfaction, reaffirming the allure and allure of this remarkable destination.

– Tapasaya, @tapasyavarmal

www.ingramcontent.com/pod-product-compliance
Lightning Source LLC
LaVergne TN
LVHW061616070526
838199LV00078B/7303